COMPANION

U.S. COINS

& CURRENCY

Allen G. Berman

©2006 Krause Publications

Published by

krause publications

An Imprint of F+W Publications

700 East State Street • Iola, WI 54990-0001
715-445-2214 • 888-457-2873

Our toll-free number to place an order or obtain
a free catalog is (800) 258-0929.

Library of Congress Catalog Number: LOC number applied for
ISBN 13-digit: 978-0-89689-401-3
ISBN 10-digit: 0-89689-401-0

Designed by Jon Stein
Edited by Dan Brownell

Printed in China

Dedication

Dedicated to the millions of private collectors, who, over the centuries, have filled our museums and deciphered our history, all for the love of knowledge.

Acknowledgments

Special thanks to the following
for providing the spectacular color
photography that made this book possible:

Coins

Heritage Numismatic Auctions, Inc.
3500 Maple Ave., 17th Floor
Dallas, TX 75219-3941
214-528-3500
800-US COINS (872-6467)
Bid@HeritageCoins.com
View full color images at Heritage Coins.com

Paper Money

Chester L. Krause

Contents

GENERAL INTRODUCTION **7**
Values. 7
Sizes 7

COIN INTRODUCTION **8**
Evolution of U.S. Coins 8
Coin Mints and Mint Marks 14
Coin Grading 15
Slabs 24
Handling and Treatment of Coins 26
To Clean or Not to Clean Coins? 26
Coin Storage 26
Coin Collecting Online 28
Coin Errors 30

COIN LISTINGS **36**
Half Cents 36

Large Cents 39
Flying Eagle Cents 44
Indian Head Cents 45
Lincoln Cents 47

Two-Cent Pieces 54

Silver Three-Cent Pieces 55
Nickel Three-Cent Pieces 57

Shield Nickels 58
Liberty Nickels 59
Buffalo Nickels 61
Jefferson Nickels 64

Bust Half Dimes 68
Seated Liberty Half Dimes 70
Bust Dimes 73
Seated Liberty Dimes 75

Barber Dimes 78
Mercury Dimes 80
Roosevelt Dimes. 82

Twenty-Cent Pieces 85

Bust Quarters 86
Seated Liberty Quarters. 88
Barber Quarters 92
Standing Liberty Quarters 94
Washington Quarters. 96
State Quarters. 101

Early Half Dollars. 111
Seated Liberty Half Dollars 115
Barber Half Dollars 120
Walking Liberty Half Dollars 123
Franklin Half Dollars 125
Kennedy Half Dollars 126

Early Silver Dollars 130
Gobrecht Dollars 132
Seated Liberty Dollars 134
Trade Dollars. 136
Morgan Dollars. 137
Peace Dollars 141
Eisenhower Dollars. 142
Susan B. Anthony Dollars. 144
Sacagawea Dollars 145

1 Dollar Gold Pieces. 147
2-1/2 Dollar Gold Pieces 150
3 Dollar Gold Pieces. 156
5 Dollar Gold Pieces. 158
10 Dollar Gold Pieces. 166
20 Dollar Gold Pieces. 173

U.S. Proof Sets 180
U.S. Mint Sets 184

PAPER MONEY INTRODUCTION **188**
Grading Paper Money 189
Handling and Treatment of Paper Money 190
Detecting Counterfeit Paper Money 190

PAPER MONEY LISTINGS **192**
Demand Notes 192
Treasury Notes 194
National Bank Notes 196
National Gold Bank Notes 205
United States Notes 206
Gold Certificates 213
Silver Certificates 217
Federal Reserve Notes 225
Federal Reserve Bank Notes 246
Confederate States Issues 250

RESOURCES **258**
Clubs and Associations 258
Museums 261
Books About U.S. Coins 262
Periodicals About U.S. Coins 267
Books About U.S. Paper Money 268

INDEX **269**

General Introduction

This book is not intended to be a comprehensive resource about coins and paper money. In fact, a full library is necessary to answer every question regarding this subject. Rather, it is intended to fill a much needed niche —a very basic introduction, in which a reader can get a quick overview of the hobby and get a general feel for the background, characteristics and values of each of the common categories presented.

Because this book is only an introduction to the subject, only brief information is given on early coins and paper money, and photos and listings focus on items from the early 1800s and later, which are the items most likely to be encountered today.

Values

Coin and currency prices can be as volatile as the stock market. While some coins and bills remain stable for years, others skyrocket during a period of popularity and then plummet when they fall out of fashion. The listings presented here simply give an idea of the normal retail value at the time of writing. Because the law of supply and demand ultimately rules, the final decision about the value of a coin lies with the buyer and seller.

Dealers are in business to make a living. This means they must pay less than the retail cost listed in this book when they are buying. Depending on the value and demand, a dealer will pay between 10 percent and 90 percent of the retail value of coins or currency listed in this reference.

Finally, the grades chosen to represent average prices are those most likely found in the market or the ones most likely to be sought by the average collector.

Sizes

Coins and paper money are not shown to scale in this book. Most coins have been enlarged to show more detail, and all paper money has been reduced to fit the pages. Thus, do not rely on the size of the photos for identification, but rather the information stamped or printed on the coins or bills, and the captions and listings accompanying them.

Coin Introduction

Evolution of U.S. Coins

An average American living in the 13 colonies during the 18th century would not have found many English silver or gold coins in his pocket. It was British policy to restrict the export of precious metals to the colonies. As a result, nothing but copper was struck for the colonies, and even that was rarely minted.

Silver coins were so scarce in the colonies that colonial Americans used any other foreign silver or gold coin that could be pressed into service. Besides Spanish coins, French, Portuguese, and occasionally German silver and gold were readily accepted when they turned up.

French Colonies 1762A Sou Marque

Some of the colonial governors also issued paper money valued in terms of discounted British currency, or in Spanish milled dollars. After the Declaration of Independence, many of the same forms of currency continued. Spanish colonial silver and gold were as popular as ever. All the new states issued their own paper money.

Because under the Articles of Confederation (the first United States Constitution) each state was essentially a fully sovereign country, some of them issued official state-sanctioned coinage.

When the Constitution took effect in 1789, it put an end to all state-issued coinage. In view of the new, stronger federal union, many people began to take the idea of a single national coinage more seriously. Others argued that it was not the place of government to get involved in such things. With the personal influence of George Washington himself

1787 Continental Congress Fugio Cent

behind them, the proponents of the new United States mint persevered, and construction began in 1792.

For both administrative and technical reasons, the mint got off to a slow start, but before the end of the year, silver five-cent pieces struck from the first president's tableware were circulating around Philadelphia. The new coinage was based on a decimal system dividing a dollar into 100 cents. The idea of the dollar as the standard unit was inspired by the Spanish piece of eight, then common in the Colonies.

Suffering under a severe shortage of both bullion and labor, as well as annual epidemics of yellow fever, the early mint never succeeded in placing substantial coinage in circulation on a national level. Broad circulation was also prevented by the rapid withdrawal and melting of much of the gold and silver coinage by speculators, because American coins had too high a precious metal content relative to their value. The endeavor became so futile that the striking of many denominations was frequently suspended. It wasn't until the 1830s that the weights of the coins were adjusted to prevent their export.

During the mint's first four decades, every die was engraved by hand, so no two looked alike. Also, the coins were struck by hand on a screw press one at a time. Finally, in 1836, the Industrial Revolution came to the U.S. Mint. Steam-powered striking equipment was imported from England. Almost overnight American coins became more neat and uniform. The old lettered edges were replaced by modern reeding, the hundreds of parallel lines found on coins today.

Also the quantities that could be produced in the same amount of time increased drastically. This technological improvement roughly coincided with the needed reduction in the coins' bullion content and with a facelift for all silver denominations. Thus, during the mid-1830s, the nation's coinage was utterly transformed.

1873 Silver Three-Cent Piece

The silver three-cent piece and three new gold denominations, $3 (1854) and $1 and $20 (1849) were introduced, partially because of the California gold rush.

1860S Gold Three Dollar Piece

But the big event of the mid-century was the coinage law of 1857. This one act eliminated the half-cent, reduced the size of the one-cent piece from bigger than a quarter to the diameter used today and, most importantly, caused foreign silver and gold to cease to be legal tender in the United States. The mint was finally able to produce enough to provide a true national coinage.

Civil War coin shortages not only resulted in many private tokens, but also inspired the two-cent and nickel three-cent pieces, and later possibly the five-cent nickel. It also saw the debut of the motto "In God We Trust" on the coinage. During the late 1860s and 1870s the nation was in the economic doldrums. Mintages were low for many denominations, particularly the silver dollar, and hence many coins are scarce today.

From the late 1870s onward, coinage was plentiful for half a century—

1885 Nickel Three-Cent Piece

sometimes too plentiful. A dominant political influence was the "Free Silver Movement," which didn't mean people wanted to be given free silver, but that they wanted unlimited quantities to be converted into coin to use up the excess that was being mined. They also intended that this increase the money supply, thereby causing inflation to erode debts.

1879O Morgan Dollar

From 1873 to 1918 and later, several laws were passed to force the government to buy silver and strike an abundance of silver dollars. Unpopular in the more developed parts of the country, the dollar coins frequently sat in government or bank vaults for decades. Minor silver also became more common during this era.

Early in the 20th century, Theodore Roosevelt led the nation to a new level of intellectual consciousness, touching on ideas as diverse as national parks and the artistic merits of the nation's coinage. For the latter, he sought the aid of the greatest sculptors of the day, deliberately looking outside the mint staff for talent. Most of the new coin designs reflect neo-

1942 Walking Liberty Half Dollar

classical artistic trends also prevalent in Europe. The beautiful designs include the Mercury dime, the Walking Liberty half, and the St. Gaudens double eagle, as well as the less classically inspired Buffalo nickel.

A commemorative coin program was also getting underway, providing an outlet for artists of various tastes. Most never saw circulation, being sold at a premium to collectors. By 1936, this had gotten so far out of hand that in that one year alone, 22 different half dollars were struck!

The need for strategic metals for armaments during World War II was the cause for interesting, if not pleasant, aberrations in the cent and nickel. The striking of these in steel and a silver-manganese alloy respectively was a response to these shortages.

1943S Zinc-Coated Steel Lincoln Cent

Idealistic images of Liberty were gradually replaced during the 1930s and 1940s with those of statesmen, and artists were determined by contests rather than by selection.

1943P Jefferson Nickel

An increase in the price of silver in 1964 prompted massive hoarding of silver coins as their content approached their face value. As a result, silver was partially or completely removed from coinage in favor of clad coinage, which can be readily distinguished by the copper core visible on the edge. Almost 30 years later, the cent, too, was debased, the bronze alloy being replaced by one of zinc simply plated with bronze.

Today, the nation's coinage is characterized by a new flood of commemoratives struck for both significant and insignificant reasons, most completely unknown to the American people. Traditionally sold at a high premium by the mint, commemoratives circulated at face value in 1999 for the first time since the Bicentennial.

2005 Oregon State Quarter

The five 1999 state quarters were the first issues in a 10-year series commemorating each state. The state quarter series has been well received by the public and has been credited with creating significant growth in the popularity of coin collecting in the U.S.

Coin Mints and Mint Marks

The first U.S. mint was constructed in Philadelphia in 1792. Over the centuries, the continuously growing facility has had several different homes in that city. Officially, all other mints are branch mints, but this does not mean that the largest quantities of each coin are always struck in Philadelphia.

The first branch mints were opened to strike coins from new gold being mined from deposits found in the South. These mints at Charlotte, North Carolina, and Dahlonega, Georgia, were opened in 1838 and closed with the Civil War in 1861. They never struck in any metal but gold, usually in small quantities. Also opened for the same duration, but of far greater importance, was the New Orleans mint. This became the second largest, striking vast numbers of coins in both gold and silver.

The San Francisco mint was opened in 1854 in response to the California Gold Rush. Today, it strikes most of the proof issues. In 1870, the silver mining boom in Nevada caused the mint to open a branch in Carson City. It was closed in 1893, and its coins are generally scarce.

Easily rivaling Philadelphia in its present importance is the Denver mint. Opened in 1906, it sometimes strikes more coins than the primary mint itself.

Recently some coins have been struck at West Point, N.Y. These are not circulation strikes, but collector issues and bullion only.

One can usually tell where a coin is struck by its mint mark, a small letter or a mark placed on the coin. In the United States, they have usually been on the reverse, but reappeared on the obverse after they were removed from 1965 to 1967. The following are mint marks used on United States coins:

none – Philadelphia
P – Philadelphia
C – Charlotte, NC
CC – Carson City, NV
D – Dahlonega, GA
D – Denver, CO
O – New Orleans, LA
S – San Francisco, CA
W – West Point, NY

Coin Grading

The value of a coin is in part determined by its "grade," or state of preservation. The most basic part of grading is determining how much a coin is worn. To describe a coin that is not present, such as in correspondence, numismatists have agreed on a series of terms to describe how much wear there is on a coin. Following are the grades from best (no wear at all) to worst (worn out):

> Uncirculated (Mint State)
> Almost Uncirculated
> Extremely Fine (Extra Fine)
> Very Fine
> Fine
> Very Good
> Good
> Fair
> Poor

For every type of U.S. and Canadian coin, very specific criteria have been agreed on for each degree of wear. For U.S. coins, these criteria were developed under the auspices of the American Numismatic Association and have been published in *Official A.N.A. Grading Standards for United States Coins,* usually called
The Gray Book. It is carried and used by virtually every coin shop. Below are some illustrations of examples of coins in each state of wear, with some of the basic requirements for that grade.

Uncirculated (Unc.) or Mint State (MS) coins, those with no wear at all, as though they had just come from the mint, have been divided into 11 basic categories, from 60 to 70, the latter being best. The reason for this is that even with no circulation at all, the coins themselves do hit each other while stored at the mint in large bags, leaving minute scuffs. These scuffs are called "bag marks." While these 11 points are a continuum, the ANA has not traditionally recognized intermediate grades other than the ones listed below. Many coin dealers do. When a legendary numismatic scholar and cataloger was asked if he could tell an MS-61 from an MS-62, he replied "No. Neither, I think, can anyone else. It is simply ammunition for those whose motivation is dishonesty and greed."

Uncirculated or Mint State coins with absolutely no bag marks or any other problems are called MS-70, but these perfect coins do not really exist for most series. To be MS-70, a coin must be fully struck and have no unpleasant stains or discoloration.

BU (Brilliant Uncirculated) refers to a mint-state coin retaining alll or most of its original luster. It may have a numeric grade of MS-60 to MS-70. In the case of higher grades, many dealers prefer to use the more precise numeric grades.

MS-67

MS-67 is the nearest thing to a perfect coin that is likely to be practically obtainable. It may have the faintest of bagmarks discernible only through a magnifying glass. Copper must have luster.

MS-65

MS-65 is a grade describing an exceptional coin. It is the highest grade that can be easily obtained when conservative grading is used. It will have no significant bag marks, particularly in open areas such as the field or the cheek. Copper may have toning. Fewer than one coin in hundreds qualifies for this grade, and is one of the most popular grade of coins with investors.

MS-63

MS-63 coins are pleasant, collectible examples that exhibit enough bag marks to be noticed, but not so many as to be considered marred, with particularly few on open areas such as the fields or a cheek.

MS-60

MS-60 describes those coins that were very much scuffed up at the mint before their release. They will often have nicks and discoloration. Sometimes called "commercial uncirculated," they may actually be less pleasant to behold than a higher grade circulated coin.

AU

About Uncirculated (AU) describes coins with such slight signs of wear that some people may in fact need a mild magnifying glass to see them. A trace of luster should be visible. One should be careful not to confuse an attractive AU coin for Uncirculated.

EF

Extremely Fine (EF, XF) is the highest grade of coin that exhibits wear significant enough to be seen easily by the unaided eye. It is a coin that still exhibits extremely clear minute detail. In the case of American coins featuring the word LIBERTY on a headband or shield, all letters must be sharp and clear. Many coins will exhibit luster, but it is not necessary.

VF

Very Fine (VF) coins show obvious signs of wear. Nevertheless, most of the detail of the design is still clear. It is an overall pleasant coin. On American coins with LIBERTY on a headband or shield, all letters must be clear.

F

Fine (F) is the lowest grade most people would consider collectible. About half the design details show for most types. On U.S. coins with LIBERTY described above, all letters must be visible if not sharp.

VG

Very Good (VG) coins exhibit heavy wear. All outlines are clear, as is generally the rim. Some internal detail also shows, but most is worn off. At least three letters of LIBERTY described above must be legible, all letters on pre-1857 copper and Morgan dollars.

G

Good (G) coins are generally considered uncollectible except for novelty purposes. The design usually shows no internal detail at all. Some of the rim may also be worn out. As described above, LIBERTY is worn off on most coins and shows just trace elements on pre-1857 copper and Morgan dollars.

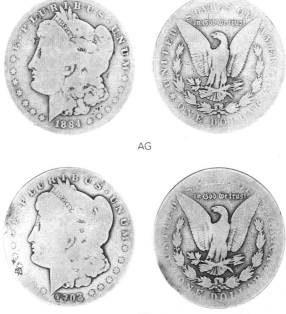

AG

FR

About Good (AG) and Fair (FR) are grades in which only truly scarce coins are collected. Many collectors would rather do without a coin than to add it to their collections. The rim will be worn down and some outline to the design may be gone.

Poor (PR) is the lowest possible grade. Many coins in Poor will not even be identifiable. When identifiable, many will still be condemned to the melting pot. Few collectors would consider owning such a coin except in the case of the most extreme rarities.

Proof

Sometimes treated as a grade, but technically not one at all is **Proof (PF)**. Proof quality is a special way of making coins for presentation. A proof coin is usually double struck with highly polished dies on polished blanks, yielding a mirror-like finish. These days, the mint mass-markets proof coins to collectors.

Ideal Toning

Poor Toning

In the past, matte or sandblast proofs were popular, characterized by a non-reflective but highly detailed surface. Cameo proof is a particular kind of proof that has been struck with dies polished only in the fields, but with the details such as the portrait deliberately given a dull finish. For some coins, these cameo proofs have a premium value above regular proofs. Proofs often grade MS-65 or higher.

Other miscellaneous factors can affect the quality of a coin. The presence of all or part of the original luster usually increases a coin's value. Be careful, however, not to be fooled by a coin that has been dipped in a brightener to simulate this luster artificially.

Toning can be good or bad. If the toning a coin has acquired is dull, irregular, or splotchy, it is likely to be considered unpleasant, and many collectors may choose to avoid it even if it is a high-grade coin.

On the other hand, if the toning is mild or displays a "halo effect" around the edge of the coin, or is composed of pleasant iridescent shades, many collectors and dealers would consider paying a premium to obtain it based on its "eye appeal." Standard phrases used to emphasize a coin's eye appeal when grading include Premium Quality (PQ) and Proof Like (PL).

Also, the mint will sometimes strike a coin on a blank that is properly prepared enough not to be considered an error, but is nevertheless in some minor way imperfect. The poor mixing of the metals in the alloy, or flaws left by trapped gas from this same process, are examples. If trivial, they may be ignored on most coins, but on more expensive or high-grade pieces, the level of concern over these flaws may increase.

Even on circulated coins, few collectors wish to have scratches or edge nicks. These will occur even more frequently on larger coins like silver dollars or on coins with reeded edges. Depending on extent, such coins may be discounted by a little or a lot.

Of course, coins with damage are worth far less than coins without. Many coins have been mounted for use in jewelry, and even when the loop or bezel has been removed, they may still show slight signs of this unfortunate experience. A few collectors consider these situations opportunities to acquire coins with high-grade detail for a fraction of the cost. It should be remembered that the same heavy discount will apply when the collector resells the coins.

SLABS

The word "slab" is numismatic slang for a tamper-resistant holder used to hold coins graded by third party grading services. Third party grading services came into existence to answer a market need particularly acute in the 1970s and early 1980s. Many investors had become aware of the impressive track records of appreciation of certain coins. Coin values were generally on the rise, and the total population of people suddenly calling themselves coin dealers was on the rise too. Many of these new dealers had as their objective to actively promote coins as investments.

With so many inexperienced customers and dealers entering the market suddenly, it became apparent that there was a dearth of knowledge. While few in the investment market were concerned if the academic numismatic knowledge was being passed along, they were very concerned that the individual either selling them their investments or buying them back may be too inexperienced or too unscrupulous to properly grade the coins. Thus, a neutral arbiter was needed: the third party grading service.

Slab Containing a 1927D 20 Dollar Gold Coin
Graded MS66 by the PCGS Grading Service

These firms examine coins and seal them in small transparent rectangular holders containing that firm's opinion of the grade. The holder does not damage the coin as embedding in Lucite would. The coin is fully removable but any attempt to remove it will cause the holder to exhibit evidence of tampering, thus preventing anyone from switching a low-grade coin into a holder indicating a high grade.

There are obvious advantages to having someone without a vested interest in the answer determine the grade of a coin, but there are disadvantages as well. While the criteria applied to coin grading, particularly to United States and Canadian coins are fairly clear and objective, no two coins wear in exactly the same manner and two individuals will not necessarily evaluate a coin in precisely the same manner.

It is quite common to send the same coin into different grading services and get significantly different answers. Sometimes this differs even in resubmitting the same coin to the same grading service. As a result, it has become common practice for dealers to review the lots of coins sent into the grading services on their return. Those coins graded too conservatively are usually broken out and resubmitted in hopes of achieving a higher grade. Those that received grades that the dealer believes to be higher than he would have assigned himself are left in the holders and sold as third party graded coins.

It is easy to see here that simply by means of attrition the population of third-party graded coins gradually becomes more and more skewed towards liberally graded coins. This does not mean that third party coins these days, or in the future are by definition misgraded, because there are always the "middle of the road" grades coming back from the services, which often are left intact, but it does mean that no collector (or investor or dealer) should blindly accept the grade printed on a plastic holder as gospel truth. There is no substitute for study, experience and examining enough coins to the point where you can make your own judgments.

There is nevertheless a market for "sight unseen" coins encapsulated in slabs. The values of such coins are determined by what the market perceives as the relative accuracy of the grading service in whose capsule the coin sits. The *Coin Dealer Newsletter* or "Graysheet" rates the relative merits of these grading services on a weekly basis. While most buyers do not pursue the sight unseen market, this quantifiable information is useful in determining which grading service to select for coins you are about to either buy or sell.

One outgrowth of the certified grading phenomenon is "population reports." Some services maintain a record of the quantity of specimens in each grade for each coin that passes through their hands. In theory this will indicate to the potential coin buyer how rarely a coin occurs in certain very high grades. These reports should be viewed with some caution. While it is officially expected that a dealer submitting a previously graded coin for regrading will indicate that it is the same coin, most do not. Hence one specimen can easily end up on the population reports as two different coins.

A peculiar reaction to the proliferation of slabs is "slab aversion" by pure collectors who have no interest in investment. This author has seen and heard of numerous instances in which collectors have refused to buy needed coins at a grade and price that pleased them purely because the coins were in slabs. There is no logical support for such conduct, as obviously anyone who finds the holder odious can throw it away. This is a rare, but observed, fact.

Handling and Treatment of Coins

How a collector treats his coins can greatly affect how well they hold their value. Metal is more reactive and softer than most people think.

The human body contains many corrosive chemicals. In some cases, simply touching a coin can contribute to its deterioration. This is especially true of coins exhibiting mint luster or iridescent toning. Touching a bright copper surface with a sweaty thumb can easily result in the appearance of a dark thumbprint several weeks or months later.

All this being said, it is easy to understand why the first lesson of coin collecting is to **never touch a coin on its surface**. If one needs to pick up a coin with bare skin, touch only its edge. In the case of proof coins, even greater precaution must be taken. The highly reflective surfaces are so sensitive that one should avoid even breathing directly on a coin. This will create small black dots that coin collectors call "carbon spots." Also, do not leave coins where they can be directly exposed to dust, sunlight, or changes in temperature.

To Clean or Not to Clean Coins?

Many new collectors ask the question "How do I remove the toning?" While it can be done, it is not recommended. While there are rare exceptions when it is beneficial, it should generally be stated that one should **never clean a coin**. It is highly likely that more harm than good will result. Toning is actually part of the coin. It is molecularly bonded to the metal, and the only way to remove the toning is to remove part of the coin. This is the way in which most coin dips work, by means of a mild acid. Physical cleaning is even worse, as microscopic striations almost inevitably are scraped into the coin's surface even using materials as mild as a tissue!

Coin Storage

Coins can be stored in many ways. One of the most convenient is in two-inch square plastic "flips." These are transparent holders with two pockets, one to contain the coin, one to contain a cardboard ticket on which information can be recorded. It folds over on itself into a size two inches by two inches. Originally, they were made only of a PVC formula plastic. This material was particularly flexible and easy to work with, but eventually it would break down, depositing a green slime on the coins it contained.

Today both the PVC formula and a new, more inert Mylar formula are available. The Mylar type is prone to cracking, but so far has not been found to damage coins. The PVC type is still popular because it is more flexible, but it is now usually used only by dealers and auction houses for temporary storage. Collectors usually repackage coins purchased in such holders before placing a coin into long-term storage.

Another common coin holder is the "two-by-two." This is a pair of cardboard squares with an adhering film of relatively inert plastic on one side. The coin is sandwiched between the two layers of plastic, and the two halves are stapled together. While this does not permit the coin to be removed and touched as easily as storage in flips, it does permit the coin to be viewed on both sides without opening the holder.

It is important to be very careful when removing coins from these holders so the coin is not accidentally scratched on the exposed ends of the staples that poke out when the holder is pulled apart. These careless staple scratches have ruined tens of thousands of good coins.

Both flips and two-by-twos fit nicely into specially made boxes. They also fit into plastic pages designed to hold 20 of either holder. The pages are transparent and will fit into most loose-leaf binders. It is important to remember not to place coins loose in the pages, as they are often of PVC plastic. Moreover, some of the thumb-cuts made to help remove the coins are large enough for some coins to fall through.

Many specialized coin folders and albums are designed not only to store and exhibit a collection, but to guide collectors. Each coin in the series is individually labeled, making the holder very convenient. It is widely believed that one of the main reasons coin collecting was able to catch on with the American middle class in the 1930s is the invention of the "penny board," a one-sheet predecessor of these modern coin folders and albums.

Old folders and albums are made by different processes than present ones. Older ones contained substances in the cardboard that tone the coins, although actual corrosion is rare. Today, most manufacturers omit these materials from their albums.

The toning also occurs with the long-term use of the orange-brown two-inch coin envelopes, although it is less of a problem with those of other colors. The toning in this case is caused by sulfur in the paper.

It is best to store a coin collection in a cool, dry environment. Of course, not everyone lives in such a climate. One common answer to this is to store a packet of silica gel in the same container as the coin collection. The gel is a desiccant and will absorb the moisture from the air. It can sometimes be obtained at photo shops, if not as easily through your local coin dealer.

COIN-COLLECTING ONLINE

It is entirely conceivable that in another few years one-third of all numismatic sales will be done over the Internet, yet at the moment, it is a secondary but growing market. Most dealers have constructed Web pages with varying results. Also there are now a couple of services which consolidate a number of dealers' offerings into a series of pages in a common location for ease of searching. At the moment, both for the dealers and for the collectors in search of dealers, the "net" is still somewhat uncharted territory. It so far lacks some of the safety mechanisms that exist with periodicals or local shops. There are no customer service awards or standard policies for advertisers, nor are there local Better Business Bureaus to which one can appeal. This does not mean there are no means by which you can discern legitimate dealers from fly-by-nights. Many of the criteria you would apply to shop, mail order, and show dealers can be applied to net dealers. Many of the more serious dealers on the "Web" also have active advertising programs in conventional media, permitting you to check with those periodicals. Also, the importance of membership in a professional organization still applies. Ask how long the dealer has been in business, not just collecting coins as a hobbyist. Perhaps the most difficult part of selecting dealers on the Web is discerning who is a legitimate, full-time numismatic expert from the skilled home computer buff with the dream of becoming a real coin dealer.

Many auction sites take no responsibility for the transactions they host, but eBay, for example, does provide one way of screening out some of the worst offenders. Stars are used to indicate the amount of customer feedback the member has. Clicking on the star gives additional information such as whether any customers have left negative comments about their transactions. While even the most honest and knowledgeable dealer may not please everybody, a dealer with more than a few percent of his feedback listed as negative should be regarded with caution. A pair of sunglasses instead of a star indicates a new ID. Some unscrupulous dealers booted off eBay have been known to simply take new identities and start over.

Whatever the medium through which a collector seeks out dealers, a collector who is willing to do some research and ask the right questions is bound to end up with a few dealers in whom he can place confidence and find a certain level of comfort.

The Internet can be used for far more than purchases. E-mail is a wonderfully immediate way to correspond. Basic computer-caution should be observed in order to avoid viruses. Never open an unexpected enclosure. Either ask the sender to post an image on a Web site, or verify that it was sent by someone you trust. Simply recognizing the return e-mail address is not enough as some viruses steal address books.

Ever more powerful search engines are making doing numismatic research a possibility. Unfortunately, too many collectors are confusing the somewhat random scattering of information on the Internet for a substitute for basic books. It does not even come close. All too often I have heard people say "I tried to look it up on the Internet and couldn't find it." This does not mean that the coin is rare. It more often means that the individual has spent hours using his computer when ten minutes with a *Standard Catalog of World Coins* would have provided a simple answer, and more likely a more accurate one.

The thousands of numismatic Web sites are a great resource. Not only do the nation's most important numismatic organizations all have Web sites, but a large minority of local coin clubs do as well. Some can even be found through the A.N.A. Web site itself. Discussion groups can also provide for interesting conversations normally only possible at larger coin shows. But remember, protect your security by not revealing an excess of personal information until you know well the trustworthiness of the individual to whom you are about to give your information. Never give out things such as passwords and home addresses. If you are convinced that a firm should be entrusted with your credit card number, send it to them in parts, contained in separate e-mails.

U.S. Government Web Sites
United States Mint: www.usmint.gov
Bureau of Engraving and Printing: www.moneyfactory.com

1863 Indian Head Cent Struck Off Center

Coin Errors

An error is a coin manufactured incorrectly or one that is manufactured correctly on damaged or incorrectly made dies. Errors have been produced by by a wide variety of mistakes, from the wrong metal being used, to the coin being struck off center. The mint tries to prevent such coins from getting out and are usually caught and melted.

Because the modern automated manufacturing process creates far fewer errors and greater uniformity than in ancient times, collectors of modern coins actually prize such mistakes. (Similar errors may actually reduce the value of ancient coins.) Errors in larger coins, proofs, and commemoratives tend to be scarcer because more attention is paid to the inspection process. Over the last 50 years, more have been getting out than in the past, and as a result, recent errors are not as valuable as early ones.

How each basic type of error occurs is explained following, along with what a typical example of such an error would retail for. Prices are for coins struck within the last 30 years. Coins may be worth more or less depending on the extent of the error. Values for most popular doubled-die cents appear in the regular listings.

Known Counterfeits: Most major doubled-die cents have been counterfeited. Virtually all examples of 1943 copper and 1944 steel cents are counterfeit. A magnet test will reveal deceptive plating, but not cleverly altered dates. Also, it is very easy to cause apparent errors by striking a coin with a coin or hammering foreign matter into it. Apparent off-metal strikes can simply be a coin plated after it was released from the mint. Some very thin coins have been bathed in acid. (Is the surface abraded?) Clipped coins are easily confused for clip errors. Almost all two-headed American coins are concoctions. Do not presume a coin is a mint error until you determine how it was made. There are thousands of such "hoax coins" out there.

Some illustrations here are of foreign coins in order to best show the effects of these errors.

(All values for error coins are for EF to MS-60 condition)

BIE Cent—A special kind of die chip in which a small chip out of the die between B and E in liberty looks like an extra letter I. Fairly common in the 1950s.......... **.25**

Blank—A blank, or planchet, is the piece of metal on which a coin is struck. Sometimes they escape the mint with no processing whatsoever. Other times they escape unstruck, but do make it through the machine that upsets the edge slightly. These are called type I and type II blanks respectively.

Cent	.50	Nickel	2.50
Dime	2.00	Quarter	4.00
Half	12.00	Dollar	30.00

Brockage—Coin struck with a coin and a die instead of two dies. Caused by the previous coin adhering to one die. If it covers the whole die, it creates a "full brockage."

Cent	13.50	Nickel	35.00
Dime	45.00	Quarter	45.00
Half	250.00	Dollar	250.00

Clashed Dies—Coin struck with a die that has been previously struck by another die, leaving some of its impression behind. On the coin, the image of the primary die will be bold, and the image of the residual impression will be very faint.

Cent	.75	Nickel	1.00
Dime	1.75	Quarter	5.50
Half	17.00	Dollar	18.00

Clip (2 types)—Coin struck on a blank that has part of its edge missing. There are two causes. A regular clip is caused by the punching device attempting to cut out the form of another coin before a previously punched blank is out of the way. A straight clip is caused when a blank is punched out from too near to the end of the sheet of metal.

Cent	.50	Nickel	2.50
Dime	2.00	Quarter	2.50
Half	10.00	Dollar	22.00

Susan B. Anthony Dollar with Cuds Caused by Major Die Breakage

Cud—A cud is a raised area of a coin near its edge. It is caused by a piece of the die chipping away. There is no striking surface in that spot to force the coin's metal down.

Cent	1.00	Nickel	3.00
Dime	3.50	Quarter	6.50
Half	22.00	Dollar	35.00

Die Chip—A die chip is similar to a cud, but it can be very small and occur anywhere in the die, not just the edge.

Cent	.25 to 1.00	Nickel	.25 to 3.00
Dime	.50 to 3.00	Quarter	2.00 to 6.00
Half	5.00 to 20.00	Dollar	5.00 to 30.00

Die Crack—A crack in the die will cause a very fine raised line across the surface of the coin it strikes. Larger cracks are worth more than values listed.

Cent	.50	Nickel	.75
Dime	.75	Quarter	1.50
Half	2.50	Dollar	6.00

This 1955 Doubled Die Lincoln Cent is Worth up to $1,500 in Circulated Grades

Doubled Die—Caused by several reasons, all in the die manufacturing process. The coins will appear blurred at first glance, but upon inspection, the details will be seen to be doubled.

Prices vary widely, from $10 to $500 or more.

1886 Double Struck Indian Head Cent

Double Struck—When a coin that has been struck fails to eject from between the pair of dies, it will receive a second impression, usually not centered.

Cent	10.00	Nickel	12.00
Dime	12.00	Quarter	40.00
Half	135.00	Dollar	400.00

Lamination—Occasionally called an "Occluded Gas Lamination," this error is caused by improper mixture of metal when the alloy is being made. It will appear as flaking on the surface.

Cent	.50	Nickel	3.00
Dime	4.00	Quarter	7.00
Half	12.00	Dollar	25.00

Mismatched Dies—This occurs when one of the two dies is that intended for another coin. To date, all but one has been struck on a blank intended for the larger coin.

Cent and Dime	**two known**	Dollar and Quarter	**47,500.00**

1904 Indian Head Cent Struck Off Center

Off Center—When the blank is not lined up with the dies, only part of the impression is made. The other part of the blank remains just that—blank!

Cent	1.00	Nickel	2.50
Dime	3.00	Quarter	8.00
Half	30.00	Dollar	40.00

Struck Through—A coin that had foreign matter on the blank, which was impressed into the surface by the die.

Cent	1.50	Nickel	1.50
Dime	1.50	Quarter	3.50
Half	9.00	Dollar	11.00

New York Statehood Quarter Struck on a Dime Planchet

Wrong Metal—When a blank intended for one coin is accidentally mixed into blanks destined for another and is struck with those dies.

Cent	100.00	Nickel	40.00
Dime	40.00	Quarter	45.00
Half	125.00	Dollar	375.00

REGULAR MINT ISSUES

HALF CENTS

The half cent is far more popular today than it ever was when it actually circulated. While they permitted very precise dealings in commerce, they were still considered a nuisance by those who had to spend them. Demand for them was very small, mintages were low, and in some years none were struck for circulation at all. They were so low a priority that the mint sometimes allocated no blanks for them, but struck them on second-hand merchant tokens instead. Even the banks didn't want them. From July 1811 until 1825 none were struck because of pressure from the banking industry. The half cent was finally abandoned in 1857.

Though not as popularly collected as the large cent, they are today considered scarce and desirable coins. Like the large cent, half cents are collected by die variety. Rare die combinations can be worth much more than common ones of the same year. Metal detector finds exhibiting porous surfaces are worth substantially less than the prices listed. Early dates are particularly difficult to find in better than well-worn condition, the Classic Head is much easier to find well preserved.

Known Counterfeits: Cheap cast replicas of the 1793 exist, as do more dangerous counterfeits of that and the 1796 "no pole" variety. Authentic half cents exist with their dates skillfully altered to resemble the rare 1831 date. The 1840s proof restrikes were actually struck by the U.S. mint in the 1850s and 1860s.

1795 Half Cent with Liberty Cap

LIBERTY CAP TYPE

	VG	VF
1793	3,250.00	7,000.00
1794	600.00	1,500.00
1795	600.00	1,500.00

	VG	VF
1796 with pole	12,000.00	20,000.00
1796 no pole	30,000.00	70,000.00
1797	600.00	1,500.00

1800 Half Cent with Draped Bust

DRAPED BUST TYPE

	VG	VF
1800	70.00	200.00
1802	1,200.00	7,000.00
1803	65.00	250.00
1804	60.00	150.00
1804 spiked chin	60.00	175.00

	VG	VF
1805	55.00	125.00
1806	55.00	125.00
1807	55.00	150.00
1808	55.00	160.00

1825 Half Cent with Classic Head

CLASSIC HEAD TYPE

	VG	VF
1809	65.00	85.00
1810	65.00	175.00
1811	225.00	1,250.00
1825	65.00	85.00
1826	65.00	85.00
1828	65.00	85.00
1829	65.00	85.00
1831	3,000.00	7,000.00

	VG	VF
1831 restrike *unc.*		6,000.00
1832	65.00	85.00
1833	65.00	85.00
1834	65.00	85.00
1835	65.00	85.00
1836 *proof only*	—	5,000.00
1836 restrike *proof only*	—	18,000.00

1849 Half Cent with Braided Hair

BRAIDED HAIR TYPE

	VG	VF
1840 *proof only*	—	4,800.00
1840 restrike *proof only*	—	4,200.00
1841 *proof only*	—	4,800.00
1841 restrike *proof only*	—	4,000.00

	VG	VF
1842 *proof only*	—	4,800.00
1842 restrike *proof only*	—	4,200.00
1843 *proof only*	—	4,800.00
1843 restrike *proof only*	—	4,200.00

	VG	VF		VG	VF
1844 *proof only*	—	4,800.00	1849 *proof only*	—	4,800.00
1844 restrike			1849 restrike		
proof only	—	4,200.00	*proof only*	—	4,200.00
1845 *proof only*	—	4,800.00	1849 large date	60.00	85.00
1845 restrike			1850	60.00	85.00
proof only	—	4,200.00	1851	60.00	85.00
1846 *proof only*	—	4,800.00	1852 *proof only*	—	60,000.00
1846 restrike			1852 restrike		
proof only	—	4,200.00	*proof only*	—	4,500.00
1847 *proof only*	—	4,800.00	1853	60.00	85.00
1847 restrike			1854	60.00	85.00
proof only	—	4,200.00	1855	60.00	85.00
1848 *proof only*	—	4,800.00	1856	60.00	85.00
1848 restrike			1857	60.00	85.00
proof only	—	4,200.00			

LARGE CENTS

The United States large cent was a result of dual desires, one for a decimal coin worth one-hundredth of a dollar. The other was the need for a coin to replace British halfpennies and their imitations, which had been common in the American colonies. It was slightly larger than the halfpenny, and the concept of decimal coinage was so innovative that the fraction "1/100" literally had to be written on the coin, along with the edge inscription "ONE HUNDRED FOR A DOLLAR."

The dies for striking early American coins had to be engraved by hand, and no two were identical. Because of this it has been very popular to collect them, especially the large cents, by die combination.

It is interesting to note that low mintages and mediocre acceptance by the public resulted in the very first large cents as being little more than local Philadelphia coinage. Metal was in such short supply that junked copper hardware of inconsistent alloy was used for some early cents, giving a poor quality blank on which to strike the coin. People also resented the chain on the first design of 1793 as a symbol antithetical to liberty, and laughed at the frightened expression they perceived on the face of Miss Liberty. Later they became so popular that they were considered good luck. In the early 1800s, they were nailed to the rafters of new houses to bring good luck to its inhabitants. These old relics, found with characteristic square nail holes through them, have a discounted value but still hold historical interest for collectors, and have been given the nickname "rafter cents." Other large cents were stamped or hand engraved with advertising, personal initials, or risqué comments, then placed back into circulation.

During the 1850s, public irritation with the heaviness of the cent began to grow and, after eight years of research into smaller alternatives, the large cent was abandoned in 1857.

Because the hand-engraved dies with which these coins were struck have been individually identified, large cents are very actively collected by die variety. Rare die combinations can be worth much more than common ones of the same year. Metal detector finds exhibiting porous surfaces are worth substantially less than the prices listed. Early dates are particularly difficult to find in better than well-worn condition.

Known Counterfeits: Large cents were not frequently counterfeited in their day. A few rarer dates were later counterfeited by casting (and possibly striking) to fool collectors. They include 1799, 1803, 1805 over 5, and 1851 over inverted 18. 1799 is also known altered from 1798. Some crude museum-souvenirs have been made of Chain Cents as well.

1793 Large Cent with Flowing Hair and Chain

1793 Large Cent with Flowing Hair and Wreath

FLOWING HAIR TYPE

	VG	VF
1793 chain Rev.	8,000.00	23,000.00
1793 wreath Rev.	2,300.00	6,000.00

1795 Large Cent with Liberty Cap (Double Struck and Rotated in Collar)

LIBERTY CAP TYPE

	VG	VF		VG	VF
1793	6,000.00	20,000.00	1795	500.00	1,300.00
1794	500.00	1,300.00	1796	500.00	1,500.00

1805 Large Cent with Draped Bust

DRAPED BUST TYPE

	VG	VF
1796	400.00	1,800.00
1797	150.00	490.00
1798	100.00	525.00
1799	3,500.00	17,000.00
1800	80.00	400.00
1801	75.00	300.00
1802	70.00	275.00
1803	70.00	275.00

	VG	VF
1804 original (open wreath)	1,400.00	3,000.00
1804 restrike (closed wreath) *unc.*	—	1,100.00
1805	60.00	300.00
1806	90.00	400.00
1807	60.00	325.00

1809 Large Cent with Classic Head

CLASSIC HEAD TYPE

	VG	VF
1808	100.00	500.00
1809	200.00	1,300.00
1810	80.00	600.00
1811	150.00	1,000.00

	VG	VF
1812	75.00	525.00
1813	95.00	600.00
1814	75.00	530.00

1828 Large Cent with Coronet

CORONET TYPE

	VG	VF		VG	VF
1816	25.00	84.00	1826	25.00	84.00
1817 13 stars	25.00	65.00	1827	25.00	75.00
1817 15 stars	25.00	125.00	1828	25.00	84.00
1818	25.00	60.00	1829	25.00	100.00
1819	25.00	63.00	1830	25.00	70.00
1820	25.00	63.00	1831	25.00	63.00
1821	40.00	400.00	1832	25.00	63.00
1822	25.00	90.00	1833	25.00	60.00
1823	110.00	675.00	1834	25.00	60.00
1823 restrike	400.00	500.00	1835	25.00	56.00
1824	25.00	145.00	1836	25.00	60.00
1825	25.00	110.00	1837	25.00	51.00

1840 Large Cent with Coronet

	VG	VF		VG	VF
1838	25.00	51.00	1844	25.00	39.00
1839	25.00	51.00	1845	25.00	39.00
1840	25.00	39.00	1846	25.00	39.00
1841	25.00	45.00	1847	25.00	39.00
1842	25.00	39.00	1848	25.00	39.00
1843	25.00	39.00	1849	25.00	39.00

	VG	VF
1850	25.00	39.00
1851	25.00	39.00
1852	25.00	39.00
1853	25.00	39.00

	VG	VF
1854	25.00	39.00
1855	25.00	39.00
1856	25.00	39.00
1857	55.00	85.00

FLYING EAGLE CENTS

After years of experimenting, the mint introduced its new small cent in 1857. It was less than half the weight of the large cent, and was brown to beige in color due to its alloy of 88 percent copper and 12 percent nickel. It depicted an eagle flying left modeled after "Old Pete," a bird which years earlier had served as a mascot at the mint. Initially these were released in certain quantities at *below face value* to encourage their acceptance, but the old large cents were so bulky that people didn't take long to convince. It's interesting to observe, in today's health-conscious atmosphere, that the wreath on the reverse contains, among other plants, tobacco.

The 1856 is technically a pattern but was widely distributed at the time, and is generally collected as part of the series.

Known Counterfeits: Most of the 1856 cents encountered are counterfeit. They are usually made from authentic coins with the dates re-engraved.

1858 Flying Eagle Cent

	VG	VF
1856	7,000.00	8,500.00
1857	24.00	44.00

	VG	VF
1858 lg. letters	24.00	45.00
1858 small letters	24.00	44.00

INDIAN HEAD CENTS

The origin of the Indian Head cent is one of the most charming in the field of numismatics. According to legend, James B. Longacre, engraver at the U.S. mint was entertaining an Indian chief who happened to be wearing his full war bonnet. As a gesture of whimsy, the chief removed his bonnet and placed it upon the head of Longacre's little girl, Sarah. The engraver instantly perceived that this was the image destined for the next American cent. Admittedly, fewer people believe this story as time goes on, but it does add a quaint bit of sentimentality to the origin of one of America's favorite coin designs.

When the Indian Head cent was first released, it was struck in the same copper-nickel alloy as the Flying Eagle cent. The reverse was a simple laurel wreath encircling the words ONE CENT. The following year this was replaced by one of oak, often considered a symbol of authority, into the bottom of which was tied a bundle of arrows. Its top was open enough to fit a small American shield.

In 1864 nickel was removed from the alloy, giving the coin the bronze appearance that has since characterized the U.S. cent. It was also made thinner like our modern cent. This new bronze cent was very reminiscent in form to the private one-cent "Civil War Tokens," which were circulating at the time, and which cost a fraction of a cent to manufacture. The mint was well aware of this obvious savings.

Known Counterfeits: Struck counterfeits of 1867, 1868, 1873 open 3, and 1877 exist. Counterfeit 1908S and 1909S are often made by altering real 1908 and 1909 Indian cents.

1859 Copper-Nickel Alloy Indian Head Cent

COPPER-NICKEL ALLOY

	F	XF
1859	20.00	100.00
1860	16.00	53.00
1861	40.00	90.00

	F	XF
1862	10.00	25.00
1863	10.00	25.00
1864	33.00	70.00

1882 Bronze Indian Head Cent

BRONZE

	F	XF
1864	20.00	60.00
1864 "L" on ribbon	125.00	250.00
1865	18.00	35.00
1866	60.00	175.00
1867	70.00	175.00
1868	50.00	160.00
1869	215.00	375.00
1870	200.00	375.00
1871	250.00	380.00
1872	230.00	400.00
1873	50.00	150.00
1874	32.00	95.00
1875	45.00	95.00
1876	60.00	200.00
1877	1,100.00	1,900.00
1878	60.00	210.00
1879	14.00	65.00
1880	6.00	25.00

	F	XF
1881	6.00	18.00
1882	6.00	18.00
1883	5.00	17.50
1884	7.00	25.00
1885	12.00	55.00
1886	18.00	120.00
1887	3.50	18.00
1888	4.00	20.00
1889	3.00	10.00
1890	3.00	10.00
1891	3.00	10.00
1892	3.75	12.00
1893	3.25	10.00
1894	9.00	42.50
1895	3.25	13.50
1896	2.75	12.00
1897	2.50	10.00

1902 Bronze Indian Head Cent

	F	XF		F	XF
1898	2.75	10.00	1905	2.00	8.00
1899	2.30	11.00	1906	1.85	8.00
1900	2.50	12.50	1907	1.85	7.50
1901	2.00	8.00	1908	2.25	8.00
1902	2.00	8.00	1908S	75.00	150.00
1903	2.00	8.00	1909	4.00	17.50
1904	2.00	8.00	1909S	400.00	525.00

LINCOLN CENTS

The Lincoln cent was the first regular issue United States coin to bear the portrait of a real person. It made its debut to celebrate the one-hundredth year of Lincoln's birth. It was designed by a sculptor from outside the mint's staff, Victor David Brenner. His initials are found prominently on the very first examples to be released. Some thought they were featured too prominently, and the outcry forced their removal, causing two varieties for the first year. Later in 1918, they were added more discretely under the truncation of the shoulder.

Lincoln cents were a bronze alloy of 95 percent copper until 1943 when they were changed to zinc-coated steel to save copper for the war effort. Because some of them were confused with dimes they were replaced in 1944 and 1945 with cents made from melted spent shell casings, resulting in a much more conventional appearance. The original alloy was restored from 1946 until 1982 when it was finally abandoned for zinc plated with copper. This was to reduce the expense of manufacturing the cent. Many people don't realize it but if you cut one of the cents struck today in half it will not be orange or brown inside but white, revealing its true composition.

A new reverse was introduced in 1959 for the 150th anniversary of Lincoln's birth and the 50th anniversary of the Lincoln cent. Still in use today, it depicts the Lincoln Memorial in Washington D.C.

The Lincoln cent is one of the most popularly collected coins on earth. It is collected in most grades, and even the rarities can be found without too long a search.

Known Counterfeits: The 1909S VDB, 1909S, 1914D, 1922-Plain, 1931S, and 1955 doubled dies have been extensively counterfeited. Most are altered cents of other dates. Counterfeits also exist of the 1972 doubled die. Virtually all 1943 bronze and 1944 steel cents are counterfeit. A magnet test will reveal the crudest counterfeits made by plating. Other 1943 bronze have been made by altering 1948 and by striking with false dies.

In addition to counterfeits, the collector should be aware of "reprocessed" cents. These are circulated 1943 steel cents given a fresh zinc coating to make them appear uncirculated. Many hobbyists are quite willing to have them in their collections, but it is important to know the difference. Don't look for luster, but look for traces of flatness at the cheekbone.

1909S VDB Lincoln Cent with Wheat Ears Reverse

WHEAT EARS REVERSE

	VF	MS-60		VF	MS-60
1909 VDB	5.25	10.00	1909S	141.75	273.00
1909S VDB	787.50	1,312.50	1910	.65	15.25
1909	2.10	14.20	1910S	14.70	65.60

	VF	MS-60
1911	1.40	18.90
1911D	14.20	84.00
1911S	26.25	157.50
1912	5.25	31.50
1912D	21.00	147.00
1912S	21.00	126.00
1913	3.70	29.40
1913D	8.90	94.50
1913S	12.60	141.75
1914	4.20	42.00
1914D	315.00	1,470.00
1914S	26.25	262.50
1915	10.50	84.00
1915D	5.25	52.50
1915S	14.20	157.50
1916	1.90	14.70

	VF	MS-60
1916D	3.70	63.00
1916S	3.70	71.40
1917	1.60	13.65
1917D	3.15	60.90
1917S	2.35	60.90
1918	1.05	12.60
1918D	2.60	63.00
1918S	2.35	63.00
1919	.80	9.45
1919D	2.30	52.50
1919S	1.80	37.80
1920	.80	12.60
1920D	2.60	57.75
1920S	2.10	84.00
1921	1.85	37.80
1921S	4.20	94.50
1922D	15.75	78.75

1922 Plain (No D) Lincoln Cent with Wheat Ears Reverse

1932D Lincoln Cent with Wheat Ears Reverse

	VF	MS-60
1922 plain	1,207.50	7,140.00
1923	1.25	12.00
1923S	5.50	185.00
1924	1.25	20.00
1924D	30.00	235.00
1924S	3.00	95.00
1925	1.00	10.00
1925D	2.00	50.00
1925S	1.50	60.00
1926	.80	8.00
1926D	1.50	60.00
1926S	7.00	110.00
1927	.80	8.00
1927D	1.25	55.00
1927S	3.50	65.00
1928	.80	8.50
1928D	1.50	30.00
1928S	2.20	65.00
1929	.80	6.00

	VF	MS-60
1929D	1.50	18.00
1929S	1.50	16.00
1930	.50	4.00
1930D	.75	12.00
1930S	.80	10.00
1931	1.40	17.50
1931D	5.00	52.00
1931S	75.00	100.00
1932	3.00	18.50
1932D	2.00	16.00
1933	2.20	17.00
1933D	3.50	18.00
1934	.25	4.00
1934D	.45	16.50
1935	.25	2.50
1935D	.30	5.50
1935S	.40	12.00
1936	.25	2.00
1936D	.25	2.75

1943 Lincoln Cents were produced with a zinc-coated steel during WWII.

	VF	MS-60
1936S	.35	2.75
1937	.20	1.75
1937D	.25	2.50
1937S	.25	3.00
1938	.20	2.00
1938D	.45	2.70
1938S	.70	2.80
1939	.20	1.00
1939D	.60	2.25
1939S	.25	1.35
1940	.25	.95
1940D	.25	1.00

	VF	MS-60
1940S	.25	1.25
1941	.15	.85
1941D	.20	2.00
1941S	.20	2.25
1942	.15	.50
1942D	.15	.50
1942S	.20	3.50
1943 steel	.30	.85
1943D steel	.35	1.00
1943S steel	.40	2.50
1944	.15	.50
1944D	.15	.45

	VF	MS-60
1944 D over S	120.00	375.00
1944S	.15	.45
1945	.15	.60
1945D	.15	.70
1945S	.15	.45
1946	.15	.35
1946D	.15	.50
1946S	.15	.50
1947	.15	.60
1947D	.15	.40
1947S	.15	.55
1948	.15	.50
1948D	.15	.45
1948S	.15	.65
1949	.15	.75
1949D	.15	.50
1949S	.15	1.00
1950	.15	.50
1950D	.15	.50
1950S	.15	.80
1951	.15	.90
1951D	.15	.50

	VF	MS-60
1951S	.15	.75
1952	.15	.50
1952D	.15	.50
1952S	.15	1.00
1953	.15	.50
1953D	.15	.50
1953S	.15	.45
1954	.15	.75
1954D	.15	.35
1954S	.15	.35
1955	.15	.30
1955 doubled die	950.00	1,550.00
1955 minor date shift or "poor man's doubled die"	.15	1.00
1955D	.15	.30
1955S	.15	.60
1956	.15	.30
1956D	.15	.30
1957	.15	.30
1957D	.15	.30
1958	.15	.30
1958D	.15	.30

LINCOLN MEMORIAL REVERSE

	BU
1959	.20
1959D	.30
1960 large date	.20
1960 small date	2.50
1960D large date	.30
1960D small date	.30
1961	.20
1961D	.20
1962	.20
1962D	.20
1963	.20
1963D	.20
1964	.20
1964D	.20
1965	.20
1966	.20
1967	.20
1968	.20
1968D	.20
1968S	.20
1969	.40

	BU
1969D	.20
1969S	.20
1970	.20
1970D	.20
1970S small date	30.00
1970S large date	.20
1971	.20
1971D	.25
1971S	.35
1972	.15
1972 doubled die	400.00
1972D	.15
1972S	.15
1973	.15
1973D	.15
1973S	.15
1974	.15
1974D	.15
1974S	.15
1975	.15
1975D	.15

	BU
1975S *proof only*	5.50
1976	.15
1976D	.15
1976S *proof only*	5.00
1977	.15
1977D	.15
1977S *proof only*	3.00
1978	.15
1978D	.15
1978S *proof only*	3.00
1979	.15

	BU
1979D	.15
1979S *proof only*	4.00
1980	.15
1980D	.15
1980S *proof only*	2.25
1981	.15
1981D	.15
1981S *proof only*	3.00
1982	.15
1982D	.15
1982S *proof only*	3.00

1982S Lincoln Cent with Lincoln Memorial Reverse

COPPER PLATED ZINC

	BU
1982	.20
1982D	.15
1983	.15
1983 doubled die rev.	300.00

	BU
1983D	.15
1983S *proof only*	4.00
1984	.15
1984 doubled die	200.00

1990S Proof, Lincoln Cent Error (Coin Struck at San Francisco Mint without S Mark)

	BU
1984D	.30
1984S *proof only*	4.50
1985	.15
1985D	.15
1985S *proof only*	5.00
1986	.30
1986D	.15
1986S *proof only*	7.50
1987	.15
1987D	.15
1987S *proof only*	5.00
1988	.15
1988D	.15
1988S *proof only*	8.00
1989	.15
1989D	.15
1989S *proof only*	3.00
1990	.15
1990D	.15
1990S *proof only*	5.75
1990 w/o S *proof only*	3,000.00
1991	.15
1991D	.15
1991S *proof only*	20.00
1992	.15
1992D	.15
1992S *proof only*	6.50
1993	.15
1993D	.15
1993S *proof only*	9.50
1994	.15
1994D	.15
1994S *proof only*	8.50
1995	.15
1995 doubled die	25.00

	BU
1995D	.15
1995S *proof only*	9.50
1996	.15
1996D	.15
1996S *proof only*	6.50
1997	.15
1997D	.15
1997S *proof only*	10.50
1998	.15
1998D	.15
1998S *proof only*	9.50
1999	.15
1999D	.15
1999S *proof only*	6.00
2000	.15
2000D	.15
2000S *proof only*	5.00
2001	.15
2001D	.15
2001S *proof only*	5.00
2002	.15
2002D	.15
2002S *proof only*	5.00
2003	.15
2003D	.15
2003S *proof only*	5.00
2004	.15
2004D	.15
2004S *proof only*	5.00
2005	.25
2005D	.25
2005S *proof only*	4.00
2006	.25
2006D	.25
2006S *proof only*	4.00

TWO-CENT PIECES

Throughout the Civil War people hoarded coins, prefering to spend the less valuable private tokens and small denomination paper money then available. If the North fell, they thought that at least real coins would retain some value. A small change shortage resulted. The two-cent piece was introduced in an attempt to alleviate this shortage. It was the first coin to carry the inscription "In God We Trust."

These are usually found well worn, fewer than one in one hundred surviving in Fine or better condition.

Known Counterfeits: Counterfeits are not particularly common, though some scarce die-struck ones are known.

1867 Two-Cent Piece

	F	XF
1864 small motto (open D in God)	200.00	550.00
1864 large motto (narrow D in God)	18.00	37.00
1865	18.00	37.00
1866	19.00	37.00
1867	20.00	38.00
1868	30.00	48.00

	F	XF
1869	30.00	53.00
1870	35.50	90.00
1871	40.00	110.00
1872	400.00	760.00
1873 closed 3 *proof only*	—	2,000.00
1873 open 3 *proof restrike*	—	2,200.00

SILVER THREE-CENT PIECES

Different times have different priorities, and the reasons for striking coins in one era don't always seem to make sense to the people living in another. This is the case of the silver three-cent piece, often called the "trime." It and the three dollar gold piece were issued to make it easier to purchase single and sheets of three-cent, first class postage stamps. Despite the extreme awkwardness of their small size, they were accepted enough in commerce that they continued to be struck in significant quantities for twelve years.

Its thinness prevented it from striking up well and the mint attempted to modify its design repeatedly. Getting a fully struck coin with no weak spots, even in higher grades is truly difficult. Another problem resulting from their thinness was their frequent bending, dents and crinkling. Prices given are for flat, undamaged examples.

Known Counterfeits: Counterfeits made to pass in circulation were struck in base silver and white metal for early dates, German silver (copper-nickel-zinc) dated 1860 and 1861. A struck counterfeit also exists for 1864.

1851O Silver Three-Cent Piece with No Border Around Star

NO BORDER AROUND STAR

	F	XF		F	XF
1851	30.00	65.00	1852	30.00	65.00
1851O	40.00	130.00	1853	30.00	65.00

1858 Silver Three-Cent Piece with Triple Border Around Star

TRIPLE BORDER AROUND STAR

	F	XF
1854	30.00	95.00
1855	55.00	165.00
1856	30.00	90.00

	F	XF
1857	30.00	90.00
1858	30.00	90.00

1863 Silver Three-Cent Piece with Double Border Around Star

DOUBLE BORDER AROUND STAR

	F	XF
1859	30.00	65.00
1860	30.00	68.00
1861	30.00	65.00
1862	30.00	65.00
1863	350.00	400.00
1864	350.00	400.00
1865	400.00	465.00
1866	350.00	400.00

	F	XF
1867	400.00	465.00
1868	400.00	465.00
1869	400.00	465.00
1870	400.00	465.00
1871	410.00	465.00
1872	430.00	500.00
1873 *proof only*	—	1,750.00

NICKEL THREE-CENT PIECES

The fact that the tiny silver three-cent piece survived at all indicated that there was some usefulness to that denomination, but its size was impractical. With Civil War silver hoarding occurring, the need for a convenient non-silver coin of this value was even more apparent. The three-cent coin was thus made bigger and changed to an alloy of 75-percent copper and 25-percent nickel, just enough nickel to give it a white color. Despite their active use in commerce for decades, they are not difficult to find well preserved.

Known Counterfeits: Few if any counterfeits of this coin are known.

1865 Nickel Three-Cent Piece

	F	XF		F	XF
1865	16.00	27.00	1878 *proof only*	—	900.00
1866	16.00	27.00	1879	77.00	95.00
1867	16.00	27.00	1880	100.00	135.00
1868	16.00	27.00	1881	16.00	27.00
1869	16.00	27.00	1882	92.00	115.00
1870	16.50	28.00	1883	200.00	280.00
1871	16.00	29.00	1884	475.00	500.00
1872	16.50	27.00	1885	550.00	600.00
1873	16.00	30.00	1886 *proof only*	—	575.00
1874	16.00	27.00	1887	275.00	325.00
1875	16.00	33.00	1888	50.00	70.00
1876	17.00	38.00	1889	100.00	120.00
1877 *proof only*	—	2,550.00			

SHIELD NICKELS

The success of the 25-percent nickel, three-cent piece emboldened the mint to strike a larger denomination in the same alloy the following year. Its design was an ornate shield, reminiscent of the then popular two-cent piece. One unfortunate characteristic of a coin struck in a hard alloy such as this is that its design is not always fully struck. In this case, not all of the horizontal shading lines are always clear, even on mint state coins. In its second year of issue the design was simplified, the rays between the stars on the reverse being removed.

Known Counterfeits: Counterfeits intended to pass in circulation were struck bearing the dates 1870 to 1876.

1866 Shield Nickel with Rays

1867 Shield Nickel with No Rays

	F	XF		F	XF
1866 rays	45.00	150.00	1875	58.00	100.00
1867 rays	50.00	190.00	1876	53.00	96.00
1867	19.00	38.00	1877 *proof only*	—	2,500.00
1868	19.00	38.00	1878 *proof only*	—	1,050.00
1869	19.00	38.00	1879	500.00	600.00
1870	33.50	62.50	1880	600.00	1,100.00
1871	85.00	200.00	1881	360.00	525.00
1872	35.00	62.50	1882	19.00	38.00
1873 closed 3	38.00	125.00	1883	26.00	48.00
1873 open 3	35.00	62.50	1883 3 over 2	250.00	480.00
1874	48.00	78.00			

LIBERTY NICKELS

The Liberty nickel had one of the most controversial beginnings of all American coins. The original design had the denomination of five cents indicated simply by the Roman numeral V, with the word cents simply understood. Or so the mint expected. However, some unprincipled persons gold plated these coins and passed them off as the new five-dollar coin. These plated frauds became known as racketeer nickels and prompted an immediate change in the coin's design. The word "cents" was added boldly underneath the large V. Today racketeer nickels have some value as collector's novelties, but not as much as a natural, unaltered coin. Interestingly the original "no cents" nickel is quite common today in medium to high grades, perhaps as an evidence of it being considered a novelty in its day.

The famous 1913 Liberty nickel is not an authorized mint issue, but was struck at the U.S. mint by a scheming employee with an eye to profit. Carefully marketed, the first advertisements to purchase these rare coins were placed by the original seller, knowing that no one else had any to sell, but knowing that this would excite interest in the numismatic community. Today, it is one of the most valuable coins in the world!

Known Counterfeits: There are counterfeits of the 1913, but they are somewhat less dangerous as all five extant pieces are in known hands. 1912S pieces exist made from altered 1912D nickels.

1896 Liberty Nickel

	F	XF
1883 no cents	7.00	9.00
1883 with cents	25.00	65.00
1884	27.50	70.00
1885	700.00	950.00
1886	340.00	575.00
1887	27.00	60.00
1888	45.00	125.00
1889	22.00	52.00
1890	23.00	56.00
1891	16.00	52.00
1892	17.50	58.00
1893	17.50	46.00

	F	XF
1894	80.00	190.00
1895	22.00	60.00
1896	30.00	68.00
1897	10.50	36.00
1898	9.50	33.00
1899	6.75	30.00
1900	6.75	30.00
1901	6.50	27.50
1902	4.50	27.50
1903	4.50	27.50
1904	4.50	28.50
1905	4.25	27.50

1907 Liberty Nickel

	F	XF
1906	4.00	27.50
1907	4.00	27.50
1908	4.00	27.50
1909	4.50	30.00
1910	4.00	25.00

	F	XF
1911	4.00	25.00
1912	4.00	25.00
1912D	7.00	65.00
1912S	225.00	750.00
1913 proof	—	3,000,000.00

BUFFALO NICKELS

The Buffalo Nickel, also called the Indian Head nickel, was one of the most artistically progressive American coins to have been struck when first issued. It was designed by James Earl Fraser, a noted sculptor of the era. Traditional belief holds that three different Indians posed for the obverse portrait, but this theory has recently been called into question. The original reverse depicting an American bison standing on a mound was changed for practical reasons the year it was issued, as the words FIVE CENTS were in such high relief that they would quickly wear off. The second reverse has the denomination in a recess below a plane on which the bison stands. The date is also rendered in high relief on these coins, and below Very Good usually wears off. Such dateless coins are of little value.

One entertaining sidelight to the Buffalo nickel is the Hobo nickel. This relic of American folk art consists of a Buffalo nickel with the portrait re-engraved by hand into a variety of different portraits. It was some individuals' way of fighting the poverty of the Great Depression, by making these works of art and selling them at a modest profit. Over the last few years they have come into their own and attempts to identify individual artists have met with some success.

Known Counterfeits: The most famous counterfeit in the series is that of the Three-legged Buffalo variety of 1937D. It should be noted that a real 3-legged buffalo can be distinguished not simply because of its missing leg, but based on numerous minor details expected where the design meets the field being missing as well. Other counterfeits are coins altered to appear to be 1913S Type II, 1918/7D, 1921S, 1924S, 1926D, and 1926S.

1913D Buffalo Nickel

	F	Unc.
1913 mound	10.00	32.00
1913D mound	19.00	60.00
1913S mound	50.00	110.00
1913 plain	9.50	32.50
1913D plain	135.00	250.00
1913S plain	375.00	550.00
1914	19.00	45.00
1914D	120.00	360.00
1914S	42.00	150.00

	F	Unc.
1915	7.00	48.00
1915D	33.00	225.00
1915S	75.00	550.00
1916	5.50	41.00
1916D	21.00	150.00
1916S	16.00	165.00
1917	5.50	55.00
1917D	35.00	315.00
1917S	65.00	365.00

1924 Buffalo Nickel

	F	Unc.
1918	5.50	95.00
1918 8 over 7	2,700.00	28,500.00
1918D	41.00	410.00
1918S	45.00	500.00
1919	2.50	45.00

	F	Unc.
1919D	55.00	540.00
1919S	45.00	510.00
1920	2.50	50.00
1920D	27.00	535.00
1920S	20.00	500.00

	F	Unc.
1921	6.75	115.00
1921S	185.00	1,500.00
1923	3.00	55.00
1923S	19.00	460.00
1924	4.00	68.00
1924D	27.50	335.00
1924S	96.00	2,250.00
1925	3.50	40.00
1925D	40.00	350.00
1925S	17.50	385.00
1926	2.25	35.00
1926D	24.00	285.00
1926S	78.00	4,500.00
1927	2.25	30.00
1927D	8.00	160.00
1927S	5.00	480.00

	F	Unc.
1928	2.25	35.00
1928D	4.00	59.00
1928S	2.25	200.00
1929	2.25	35.00
1929D	2.25	55.00
1929S	2.00	45.00
1930	2.25	29.00
1930S	2.25	43.00
1931S	16.00	45.00
1934	2.25	48.00
1934D	2.35	75.00
1935	1.10	19.00
1935D	2.00	67.00
1935S	1.10	49.00
1936	1.00	15.00

1937D "Three-Legged" Buffalo

	F	Unc.
1936D	1.00	34.00
1936S	1.00	34.00
1937	1.00	14.00
1937D	1.00	18.00

	F	Unc.
1937D 3-legged	700.00	2,300.00
1937S	1.00	24.00
1938D	2.00	17.00
1938D D over S	10.00	45.00

JEFFERSON NICKELS

The Jefferson Nickel was the first circulating United States coin to be designed by public contest. Felix Schlag won $1,000 for his design featuring Jefferson's portrait on one side, and his home Monticello on the other. The initial rendition lacks the designer's initials, which were not added until 1966.

During World War II nickel was needed for the war effort, so from mid-1942 to the end of 1945 "nickels" were struck in an unusual alloy of 56-percent copper, 35-percent silver and 9-percent manganese. These War Nickels bear a large mint mark over the dome. These coins exhibit great brilliance when new, but quickly turn an ugly dull color with a moderate amount of wear.

A pair of special nickels were issued to circulation in 2004, struck to commemorate the bicentennial of the expedition of exploration, from St. Louis to the Pacific, led by Meriwether Lewis and William Clark. They bear the standard Jefferson obverse. One reverse bears clasped hands adapted from a Jefferson era Indian peace medal. The other shows an old keelboat used for navigating rivers.

Due to the difficulty of getting the metal to flow into every crevice of the die, many coins are struck with the steps of Monticello on the standard reverse incompletely struck. Full step nickels sometimes command a premium from specialists.

Known Counterfeits: 1950D. Crude casts were also made to circulate in the 1940s.

1939 Jefferson Nickel

	VF	BU
1938	.80	4.00
1938D	1.25	3.50
1938S	2.00	4.00
1939	.25	1.75
1939D	5.00	38.00
1939S	1.50	15.00
1940	.25	1.00
1940D	.30	1.50
1940S	.25	2.50
1941	.25	1.00
1941D	.30	2.50
1941S	.30	3.75
1942	.25	5.00
1942D	.60	27.00

WARTIME SILVER ALLOY

	VF	BU
1942P	1.00	6.00
1942S	1.10	6.00
1943P	1.00	2.75
1943P 3 over 2	40.00	175.00
1943D	1.50	3.00
1943S	1.00	3.00
1944P	1.00	3.00
1944D	1.00	6.50
1944S	1.25	3.50
1945P	1.00	3.50
1945D	1.00	3.50
1945S	.80	2.60

REGULAR ALLOY

	VF	BU
1946	.25	.80
1946D	.25	.85
1946S	.30	.50
1947	.25	.75
1947D	.25	.90
1947S	.25	.80
1948	.25	.50
1948D	.25	1.20
1948S	.25	1.00
1949	.25	1.25
1949D	.30	1.00
1949D D over S	40.00	170.00
1949S	.45	1.50
1950	.35	1.50
1950D	6.00	8.50
1951	.40	1.25
1951D	.40	1.45
1951S	.50	1.75

	VF	BU
1952	.25	.85
1952D	.30	1.50
1952S	.25	.75
1953	.25	.40
1953D	.25	.40
1953S	.25	.50
1954	.25	.35
1954D	.25	.35
1954S	.25	.50
1954S S over D	9.00	22.00
1955	.40	.75
1955D	—	.35
1955D D over S	8.50	33.00
1956	—	.25
1956D	—	.25
1957	—	.25
1957D	—	.25
1958	—	.30
1958D	—	.25
1959	—	.30
1959D	—	.25
1960	—	.25
1960D	—	.25
1961	—	.25
1961D	—	.25
1962	—	.25
1962D	—	.25
1963	—	.25
1963D	—	.25
1964	—	.25
1964D	—	.25
1965	—	.25
1966	—	.25
1967	—	.25
1968D	—	.25
1968S	—	.25
1969D	—	.25
1969S	—	.25
1970D	—	.25
1970S	—	.25
1971	—	.75
1971D	—	.25
1971S proof only	—	1.60
1972	—	.25
1972D	—	.25
1972S proof only	—	2.00
1973	—	.25
1973D	—	.25

1965 Regular Alloy Jefferson Nickel

	VF	BU		VF	BU
1973S *proof only*	—	**1.75**	1980D	—	.25
1974	—	.25	1980S *proof only*	—	1.50
1974D	—	.25	1981P	—	.25
1974S *proof only*	—	2.00	1981D	—	.25
1975	—	.25	1981S *proof only*	—	2.00
1975D	—	.25	1982P	—	1.00
1975S *proof only*	—	2.25	1982D	—	1.25
1976	—	.25	1982S *proof only*	—	3.00
1976D	—	.25	1983P	—	1.50
1976S *proof only*	—	2.00	1983D	—	1.00
1977	—	.25	1983S *proof only*	—	4.00
1977D	—	.25	1984P	—	1.25
1977S *proof only*	—	1.75	1984D	—	.25
1978	—	.25	1984S *proof only*	—	5.00
1978D	—	.25	1985P	—	.30
1978S *proof only*	—	1.75	1985D	—	.30
1979	—	.25	1985S *proof only*	—	4.00
1979D	—	.25	1986P	—	.30
1979S *proof only*	—	1.50	1986D	—	.85
1980P	—	.25			

2004P Jefferson Nickel with Peace Reverse

2004D Jefferson Nickel with Lewis and Clark Keelboat Reverse

	VF	BU		VF	BU
1986S proof only	—	7.00	1993P	—	.25
1987P	—	.25	1993D	—	.25
1987D	—	.25	1993S proof only	—	4.00
1987S proof only	—	3.50	1994P	—	.25
1988P	—	.25	1994P matte finish	—	75.00
1988D	—	.25	1994D	—	.25
1988S proof only	—	5.50	1994S proof only	—	4.00
1989P	—	.25	1995P	—	.25
1989D	—	.25	1995D	—	.35
1989S proof only	—	4.50	1995S proof only	—	6.50
1990P	—	.25	1996P	—	.25
1990D	—	.25	1996D	—	.25
1990S proof only	—	5.50	1996S proof only	—	3.00
1991P	—	.25	1997P	—	.25
1991D	—	.25	1997P matte finish	—	200.00
1991S proof only	—	5.00	1997D	—	.25
1992P	—	.75	1997S proof only	—	5.00
1992D	—	.25	1998P	—	.25
1992S proof only	—	4.00	1998D	—	.25

2005D Jefferson Nickel with Buffalo Reverse

2006D Jefferson Nickel with Large Head Facing Obverse/
Enhanced Monticello Reverse

	VF	BU
1998S *proof only*	—	4.50
1999P	—	.25
1999D	—	.25
1999S *proof only*	—	3.50
2000P	—	.25
2000D	—	.25
2000S *proof only*	—	2.00
2001P	—	.30
2001D	—	.30
2001S *proof only*	—	2.00
2002P	—	.25
2002D	—	.25
2002S *proof only*	—	2.00
2003P	—	.30
2003D	—	.30
2003S *proof only*	—	2.00
2004P peace rev.	—	.35
2004D peace rev.	—	.35

	VF	BU
2004S peace rev. *proof only*	—	8.00
2004P keelboat rev.	—	.35
2004D keelboat rev.	—	.35
2004S keelboat rev. *proof only*	—	8.00
2005P Buffalo rev	—	.65
2005D Buffalo rev.	—	.65
2005S Buffalo rev. *proof only*	—	3.00
2005P Pacific Coastline rev.	—	.65
2005D Pacific Coastline rev.	—	.65
2005S Pacific Coastline rev., *proof only*	—	3.00
2006P Large head facing/enhanced Monticello	—	.65
2006D Large head facing/enhanced Monticello	—	.65
2006S Large head facing/enhanced Monticello *proof only*	—	4.00

BUST HALF DIMES

The United States did not always have nickel five-cent pieces. The original ones were very small silver coins called half dimes. Their designs almost always resembled those used on large whole dimes. Despite it being a priority of George Washington, half dimes were not consistently struck in early America. Between 1805 and 1829 none were struck at all.

The bust half dime's thinness resulted in frequent bending and dents. Prices given are for flat, undamaged examples. Rare die combinations of early specimens command a premium from specialists.

Known Counterfeits: 1795.

1794 Half Dime with Flowing Hair

1796 Half Dime with Draped Bust and Small Eagle

FLOWING HAIR TYPE			DRAPED BUST/SMALL EAGLE		
	VG	VF		VG	VF
1794	1,200.00	2,700.00	1796	1,350.00	3,500.00
1795	900.00	2,000.00	1797	1,250.00	3,250.00

1800 Half Dime with Draped Bust and Heraldic Eagle

1829 Half Dime with Capped Bust

DRAPED BUST/HERALDIC EAGLE

	VG	VF
1800	800.00	2,500.00
1801	1,150.00	2,800.00
1802	25,000.00	65,000.00
1803	950.00	2,200.00
1805	1,250.00	2,500.00

CAPPED BUST TYPE

	VG	VF
1829	36.00	75.00
1830	36.00	75.00
1831	36.00	75.00
1832	36.00	75.00
1833	36.00	75.00
1834	36.00	75.00
1835	36.00	75.00
1836	36.00	75.00
1837	36.00	75.00

SEATED LIBERTY HALF DIMES

Following the introduction of the Seated Liberty design by Christian Gobrecht on the silver dollar, the smaller coins were gradually brought into harmony with this design. It is generally accepted that the seated goddess version of Liberty was directly or indirectly inspired by depictions of the Roman allegory of Britannia on British coins. The half dime and dime, because of their small size, were redesigned to have a laurel wreath encircling the denomination on the reverse, rather than an eagle.

There were several minor changes over the life of this coin. After only a year the plain obverse was ornamented by 13 stars. Two years later additional drapery was added below Liberty's elbow. The arrows by the date from 1853 to 1855 indicate a 7½ percent reduction in weight. A far more obvious design change was the shift of the words UNITED STATES OF AMERICA from the reverse to the obverse in 1860.

The seated half dime's thinness resulted in frequent bending and dents. Prices given are for flat, undamaged examples.

Known Counterfeits: Counterfeit half dimes are not frequently encountered.

1837 Seated Liberty Half Dime with Plain Obverse Field

SEATED LIBERTY—
PLAIN OBVERSE FIELD

	VG	VF		VG	VF
1837	35.00	100.00	1838O	125.00	400.00

1855O Seated Liberty Half Dime with Stars and Arrows on Obverse

SEATED LIBERTY—
STARS ON OBVERSE

	VG	VF		VG	VF
1838	19.00	26.00	1840O	19.00	50.00
1839	19.00	29.00	1841	19.00	26.00
1839O	19.00	35.00	1841O	19.00	42.00
1840	19.00	26.00	1842	19.00	26.00

	VG	VF
1842O	45.00	225.00
1843	19.00	26.00
1844	19.00	26.00
1844O	105.00	450.00
1845	19.00	26.00
1846	450.00	1,150.00
1847	19.00	26.00
1848	19.00	26.00
1848O	25.00	50.00
1849	19.00	26.00
1849 overdates	19.00	40.00
1849O	40.00	225.00
1850	19.00	26.00
1850O	19.00	50.00
1851	19.00	26.00
1851O	19.00	35.00
1852	19.00	26.00

	VG	VF
1852O	32.00	135.00
1853 no arrows	36.00	100.00
1853O no arrows	260.00	675.00
1853 arrows	19.00	26.00
1853O arrows	19.00	26.00
1854	19.00	26.00
1854O	19.00	26.00
1855	19.00	26.00
1855O	20.00	55.00
1856	19.00	26.00
1856O	19.00	38.00
1857	19.00	26.00
1857O	19.00	33.00
1858	19.00	26.00
1858O	19.00	36.00
1859	19.00	34.00
1859O	19.00	40.00

1863 Seated Liberty Half Dime with Legend on Obverse

SEATED LIBERTY—
LEGEND ON OBVERSE

	VG	VF
1860	19.00	26.00
1860O	19.00	26.00
1861	19.00	26.00
1862	19.00	26.00
1863	225.00	375.00
1863S	35.00	75.00
1864	425.00	600.00
1864S	65.00	150.00
1865	400.00	550.00
1865S	35.00	75.00
1866	450.00	650.00
1866S	35.00	75.00
1867	550.00	800.00

	VG	VF
1867S	35.00	75.00
1868	70.00	170.00
1868S	25.00	40.00
1869	25.00	40.00
1869S	22.00	35.00
1870	22.00	35.00
1870S		unique
1871	13.00	26.00
1871S	30.00	60.00
1872	13.00	26.00
1872S	13.00	26.00
1873	13.00	26.00
1873S	25.00	40.00

BUST DIMES

Due to limited mint capacity dimes were not struck until 1796, even though other denominations of United States silver began to be struck two years earlier. Dime production was suspended occasionally when enough small Mexican coins were imported to satisfy demanad. The initial reverse design, which showed a rather skinny eagle within a wreath, was replaced after two more years with a plumper eagle carrying a heraldic shield. In 1809 a cap was added to Liberty and her bust was turned to the left. In the same year a denomination first appeared, not as "dime" however but as "10C." Rare die combinations of early specimens command a premium from specialists.

Known Counterfeits: Scarce cast counterfeits are known.

1796 Dime with Draped Bust and Small Eagle

DRAPED BUST/SMALL EAGLE

	VG	VF
1796	1,950.00	3,250.00
1797 13 stars	1,950.00	3,250.00
1797 16 stars	1,950.00	3,250.00

1807 Dime with Draped Bust and Heraldic Eagle

DRAPED BUST/HERALDIC EAGLE

	VG	VF		VG	VF
1798 over 97, 13 stars	2,500.00	6,000.00	1803	700.00	1,500.00
1798 over 97, 16 stars	800.00	1,500.00	1804, 13 stars	1,900.00	5,500.00
1798	925.00	2,000.00	1804, 14 stars	2,100.00	6,000.00
1800	800.00	1,600.00	1805	650.00	1,050.00
1801	850.00	2,500.00	1807	650.00	1,050.00
1802	1,400.00	3,000.00			

1830/29 Dime with Capped Bust

CAPPED BUST TYPE

	VG	VF		VG	VF
1809	200.00	650.00	1828 large date	110.00	365.00
1811 over 9	165.00	550.00	1828 small date	45.00	195.00
1814 small date	70.00	400.00	1829 (varieties)	35.00	70.00
1814 large date	35.00	200.00	1830 30 over 29	60.00	250.00
1820	35.00	150.00	1830	35.00	65.00
1821 small date	35.00	175.00	1831	35.00	60.00
1821 large date	35.00	150.00	1832	35.00	60.00
1822	600.00	1,650.00	1833	35.00	62.00
1823, 3 over 2	35.00	150.00	1834	35.00	60.00
1824, 4 over 2	50.00	400.00	1835	35.00	60.00
1825	35.00	150.00	1836	35.00	60.00
1827	35.00	140.00	1837	35.00	60.00

SEATED LIBERTY DIMES

Following the introduction of the Seated Liberty design by Christian Gobrecht on the silver dollar, the smaller coins were gradually brought into harmony with this design. It is generally accepted that the seated goddess version of Liberty was directly or indirectly inspired by depictions of the Roman allegory of Britannia on British coins. The dime and half dime, because of their small size, were redesigned to have a laurel wreath encircling the denomination on the reverse, rather than an eagle.

There were several minor changes over the life of this coin. After somewhat more than a year the plain obverse was ornamented by 13 stars. A year later, additional drapery was added below Liberty's elbow. The arrows by the date from 1853 to 1855 indicate a 7 percent reduction in weight, those in 1873 to 1874 a minuscule increase. A far more obvious design change was the shift of the words UNITED STATES OF AMERICA from the reverse to the obverse in 1860.

The seated dime's thinness resulted in frequent bending and dents. Prices given are for flat, undamaged examples.

Known Counterfeits: Collector counterfeits of seated dimes are not frequently encountered, but circulating counterfeits were struck in copper, lead, and white metal (tin and lead alloys), particularly during the 1850s-1860s.

1837 Seated Liberty Dime with Plain Obverse Field

**SEATED LIBERTY—
OBVERSE FIELD PLAIN**

	VG	VF		VG	VF
1837	40.00	275.00	1838O	45.00	300.00

1844 Seated Liberty Dime with Stars on Obverse

SEATED LIBERTY—
STARS ON OBVERSE

	VG	VF
1838 (varieties)	18.00	25.00
1839	18.00	35.00
1839O	18.00	45.00
1840	18.00	30.00
1840O	22.00	70.00
1840 extra drapery from elbow	45.00	185.00
1841	18.00	25.00
1841O	18.00	30.00
1842	18.00	23.00
1842O	18.00	75.00
1843	18.00	23.00
1843O	65.00	275.00
1844	350.00	800.00
1845	18.00	23.00
1845O	35.00	200.00
1846	200.00	400.00
1847	25.00	75.00
1848	20.00	45.00
1849	18.00	28.00
1849O	30.00	120.00
1850	18.00	25.00

	VG	VF
1850O	25.00	70.00
1851	18.00	23.00
1851O	25.00	75.00
1852	18.00	23.00
1852O	30.00	125.00
1853 no arrows	90.00	195.00
1853 arrows	18.00	23.00
1853O arrows	18.00	45.00
1854	18.00	23.00
1854O	18.00	25.00
1855	18.00	23.00
1856	18.00	23.00
1856O	18.00	35.00
1856S	225.00	500.00
1857	18.00	23.00
1857O	18.00	25.00
1858	18.00	35.00
1858O	25.00	85.00
1858S	150.00	425.00
1859	20.00	45.00
1859O	20.00	45.00
1859S	200.00	500.00
1860S	40.00	135.00

SEATED LIBERTY—
LEGEND ON OBVERSE

	VG	VF
1860	22.00	31.00

	VG	VF
1860O	475.00	1,650.00

1877 Seated Liberty Dime with Legend on Obverse

	VG	VF		VG	VF
1861	18.00	23.00	1874S arrows	70.00	160.00
1861S	85.00	275.00	1875	18.00	23.00
1862	18.00	25.00	1875CC	18.00	23.00
1862S	60.00	175.00	1875S	18.00	23.00
1863	450.00	700.00	1876	18.00	23.00
1863S	40.00	125.00	1876CC	18.00	23.00
1864	425.00	650.00	1876S	18.00	23.00
1864S	35.00	95.00	1877	18.00	23.00
1865	450.00	750.00	1877CC	18.00	23.00
1865S	45.00	125.00	1877S	18.00	30.00
1866	500.00	800.00	1878	18.00	23.00
1866S	50.00	145.00	1878CC	75.00	190.00
1867	700.00	1,100.00	1879	250.00	385.00
1867S	50.00	125.00	1880	215.00	300.00
1868	22.00	40.00	1881	225.00	325.00
1868S	30.00	80.00	1882	18.00	23.00
1869	30.00	75.00	1883	18.00	23.00
1869S	25.00	45.00	1884	18.00	23.00
1870	22.00	38.00	1884S	35.00	65.00
1870S	350.00	550.00	1885	18.00	23.00
1871	20.00	33.00	1885S	475.00	1,450.00
1871CC	1,850.00	4,000.00	1886	18.00	23.00
1871S	55.00	115.00	1886S	55.00	95.00
1872	18.00	23.00	1887	18.00	23.00
1872CC	650.00	2,000.00	1887S	18.00	23.00
1872S	60.00	150.00	1888	18.00	23.00
1873 closed 3	18.00	27.00	1888S	18.00	25.00
1873 open 3	30.00	60.00	1889	18.00	23.00
1873CC		Unique	1889S	18.00	35.00
1873 arrows	18.00	50.00	1890	18.00	23.00
1873CC arrows	1,850.00	4,000.00	1890S	18.00	50.00
1873S arrows	30.00	70.00	1891	18.00	23.00
1874 arrows	18.00	50.00	1891O	18.00	23.00
1874CC arrows	5,500.00	12,500.00	1891S	18.00	25.00

BARBER DIMES

The dime, quarter, and half dollar introduced in 1892 bear a portrait head of Liberty instead an entire figure. They were designed by Chief Engraver Charles E. Barber, after whom they have been popularly named. More practical than artistically adventurous, contemporaries thought the design rather boring if not unpleasant. Because of its small size, the dime differed from the other two denominations in the Barber series in that the reverse simply has the value within a wreath, rather than an eagle, much as occurred with the Seated Liberty coinage.

Known Counterfeits: The rare 1894S has certainly been counterfeited.

1898S Barber Dime

	F	XF		F	XF
1892	16.00	24.00	1896O	265.00	400.00
1892O	27.00	50.00	1896S	280.00	345.00
1892S	175.00	245.00	1897	6.50	24.00
1893, 3 over 2	75.00	275.00	1897O	250.00	400.00
1893	17.50	35.00	1897S	90.00	120.00
1893O	110.00	150.00	1898	6.50	21.50
1893S	25.00	55.00	1898O	80.00	180.00
1894	100.00	145.00	1898S	26.00	58.00
1894O	190.00	330.00	1899	6.50	20.00
1894S *very rare proof*	125,000.00		1899O	68.00	125.00
1895	300.00	485.00	1899S	19.50	40.00
1895O	715.00	1,950.00	1900	6.50	21.50
1895S	120.00	195.00	1900O	95.00	200.00
1896	50.00	83.00	1900S	9.50	23.00

1903S Barber Dime

	F	XF		F	XF
1901	5.75	20.00	1908O	42.50	72.00
1901O	12.00	42.00	1908S	9.00	35.00
1901S	340.00	420.00	1909	3.50	20.00
1902	4.50	20.00	1909D	58.00	115.00
1902O	13.00	42.50	1909O	9.50	28.00
1902S	52.00	95.00	1909S	83.00	165.00
1903	3.50	20.00	1910	3.50	20.00
1903O	9.75	26.00	1910D	7.75	36.00
1903S	335.00	800.00	1910S	47.00	90.00
1904	6.00	20.00	1911	3.00	20.00
1904S	140.00	270.00	1911D	3.75	20.00
1905	4.50	20.00	1911S	7.75	34.00
1905O	30.00	60.00	1912	2.75	20.00
1905S	6.00	32.00	1912D	3.75	20.00
1906	3.50	20.00	1912S	5.50	29.00
1906D	8.00	29.00	1913	2.75	20.00
1906O	44.00	85.00	1913S	75.00	195.00
1906S	10.00	39.00	1914	3.00	20.00
1907	3.50	20.00	1914D	3.50	20.00
1907D	7.50	34.00	1914S	7.25	35.00
1907O	29.00	55.00	1915	3.00	20.00
1907S	11.00	42.00	1915S	30.00	55.00
1908	3.50	20.00	1916	3.25	20.00
1908D	5.50	28.00	1916S	4.75	20.00

MERCURY DIMES

The name Mercury for this dime is a misnomer. Designed by Adolph Weinman, it actually depicts Liberty wearing a winged cap, representing freedom of thought. It was received with wide acclaim for its artistic merit when it was first released as part of a program for the beautification of United States coinage. The reverse carries the ancient Roman fasces, a symbol of authority still seen in the United States Senate. The horizontal bands tying the fasces together do not always strike up distinctly from each other, and those coins with "full split bands" often command a premium.

Known Counterfeits: These include 1916D, 1921, 1921D, 1931D, 1942/1, 1942/1D, most of which have been made by altering the mint mark on a more common date. The date 1923D is a fantasy, none having been struck.

1916D Mercury Dime

	VF	MS-60		VF	MS-60
1916	6.00	30.00	1919S	13.00	175.00
1916D	2,650.00	6,300.00	1920	3.50	27.50
1916S	8.00	35.00	1920D	7.00	105.00
1917	4.75	28.00	1920S	7.00	110.00
1917D	21.00	120.00	1921	260.00	1,000.00
1917S	5.50	62.00	1921D	335.00	1,100.00
1918	10.00	70.00	1923	3.50	27.50
1918D	9.50	105.00	1923S	12.00	160.00
1918S	8.00	90.00	1924	4.25	42.00
1919	5.00	37.00	1924D	13.00	160.00
1919D	20.00	175.00	1924S	8.75	170.00

1925D Mercury Dime

1942 Mercury Dime

	VF	MS-60		VF	MS-60
1925	4.00	28.00	1931S	6.00	84.00
1925D	36.00	350.00	1934	3.00	20.00
1925S	11.50	175.00	1934D	4.00	45.00
1926	2.75	25.00	1935	2.15	8.00
1926D	8.00	110.00	1935D	3.75	34.00
1926S	45.00	870.00	1935S	3.00	24.00
1927	3.50	26.00	1936	2.25	8.00
1927D	18.00	175.00	1936D	3.00	26.00
1927S	7.75	280.00	1936S	2.50	20.00
1928	3.50	27.50	1937	2.00	8.00
1928D	17.00	170.00	1937D	3.00	21.00
1928S	5.50	110.00	1937S	3.00	24.00
1929	2.75	20.00	1938	2.25	13.00
1929D	6.00	25.00	1938D	3.50	16.00
1929S	4.00	32.50	1938S	2.35	20.00
1930	3.50	26.00	1939	2.00	8.50
1930S	5.50	70.00	1939D	2.00	7.50
1931	4.25	35.00	1939S	2.50	21.00
1931D	15.00	84.00	1940	1.10	6.00

	VF	MS-60
1940D	1.10	7.00
1940S	1.10	7.00
1941	1.10	5.00
1941D	1.10	7.00
1941S	1.10	7.00
1942, 2 over 1	715.00	1,900.00
1942D, 2 over 1	680.00	1,900.00
1942	1.10	5.50
1942D	1.10	7.00
1942S	1.10	9.00

	VF	MS-60
1943	1.10	5.50
1943D	1.10	7.50
1943S	1.10	8.25
1944	1.10	5.50
1944D	1.10	6.00
1944S	1.10	6.50
1945	1.10	4.00
1945D	1.10	4.50
1945S	1.10	6.50
1945S micro S	3.00	23.00

ROOSEVELT DIMES

The fact that the dime was chosen to bear the image of Franklin Roosevelt is not a coincidence. It was selected to remind people of the President's involvement in the March of Dimes. He himself was crippled by polio. The coin was designed on a tight deadline by Chief Engraver John R. Sinnock. There are no true rarities in this series.

Known Counterfeits: Counterfeit Roosevelt dimes are quite rare.

1964 Roosevelt Dime (Silver)

	XF	BU
1946	1.00	1.75
1946D	1.00	1.75
1946S	1.00	2.50
1947	1.00	3.50
1947D	1.00	4.00
1947S	1.00	4.00
1948	1.00	4.00
1948D	1.20	2.50

	XF	BU
1948S	.95	2.00
1949	1.50	15.00
1949D	1.25	4.50
1949S	2.75	35.00
1950	.95	3.00
1950D	.65	3.00
1950S	1.25	30.00
1950S, S over D	70.00	225.00

1968 Roosevelt Dime (Cupro-Nickel Clad Copper)

	XF	BU
1951	1.00	1.75
1951D	1.00	1.75
1951S	1.05	10.00
1952	1.00	1.65
1952D	1.00	1.35
1952S	1.05	4.00
1953	1.00	1.35
1953D	1.00	1.35
1953S	1.00	1.35
1954	1.00	1.35
1954D	1.00	1.35
1954S	1.00	1.35
1955	1.00	1.35
1955D	1.00	1.35
1955S	1.00	1.35
1956	1.00	1.35
1956D	1.00	1.35

	XF	BU
1957	.60	1.00
1957D	.60	1.00
1958	.60	1.00
1958D	.60	1.00
1959	.60	1.00
1959D	.60	1.00
1960	.60	1.00
1960D	.60	1.00
1961	.60	1.00
1961D	.60	1.00
1962	.60	1.00
1962D	.60	1.00
1963	.60	.95
1963D	.60	.95
1964	.60	.90
1964D	.60	.90

CUPRO-NICKEL CLAD COPPER

	XF	BU
1965	—	.60
1966	—	.50
1967	—	.50
1968	—	.50
1968D	—	.50
1968S *proof only*	—	.75
1969	—	.50
1969D	—	.50
1969S *proof only*	—	.75
1970	—	.50
1970D	—	.50
1970S *proof only*	—	.75
1971	—	.50

	XF	BU
1971D	—	.50
1971S *proof only*	—	.75
1972	—	.50
1972D	—	.50
1972S *proof only*	—	1.00
1973	—	.50
1973D	—	.40
1973S *proof only*	—	1.00
1974	—	.40
1974D	—	.40
1974S *proof only*	—	1.25
1975	—	.50
1975D	—	.40

	XF	BU		XF	BU
1975S *proof only*	—	1.50	1991P	—	.35
1976	—	.50	1991D	—	.35
1976D	—	.50	1991S *proof only*	—	3.25
1976S *proof only*	—	1.00	1992P	—	.35
1977	—	.40	1992D	—	.35
1977D	—	.40	1992S *proof only*	—	3.40
1977S *proof only*	—	1.75	1992S Silver, *proof only*	—	4.25
1978	—	.40	1993P	—	.35
1978D	—	.40	1993D	—	.35
1978S *proof only*	—	1.25	1993S *proof only*	—	5.85
1979	—	.40	1993S Silver, *proof only*	—	7.50
1979D	—	.40	1994P	—	.35
1979 thick S *proof only*	—	1.00	1994D	—	.35
1979 thin S *proof only*	—	1.25	1994S *proof only*	—	5.00
1980P	—	.40	1994S Silver, *proof only*	—	7.00
1980D	—	.40	1995	—	.35
1980S *proof only*	—	1.00	1995D	—	.35
1981P	—	.40	1995S *proof only*	—	5.00
1981D	—	.40	1995S Silver, *proof only*	—	7.00
1981S *proof only*	—	1.00	1996	—	.35
1982P	—	1.00	1996D	—	.35
1982 no mint mark error	50.00	125.00	1996W	—	12.00
1982D	—	.50	1996S *proof only*	—	2.50
1982S *proof only*	—	1.25	1996S Silver, *proof only*	—	7.50
1983P	—	.50	1997P	—	.35
1983D	—	.50	1997D	—	.35
1983S *proof only*	—	1.25	1997S *proof only*	—	8.00
1984P	—	.35	1997S Silver, *proof only*	—	20.00
1984D	—	.50	1998P	—	.35
1984S *proof only*	—	1.60	1998D	—	.35
1985P	—	.50	1998S *proof only*	—	4.00
1985D	—	.40	1998S Silver, *proof only*	—	8.00
1985S *proof only*	—	1.10	1999P	—	.35
1986P	—	.50	1999D	—	.35
1986D	—	.35	1999S *proof only*	—	3.00
1986S *proof only*	—	2.50	1999S Silver, *proof only*	—	5.00
1987P	—	.35	2000P	—	.35
1987D	—	.35	2000D	—	.35
1987S *proof only*	—	1.25	2000S *proof only*	—	2.00
1988P	—	.35	2000S Silver, *proof only*	—	5.00
1988D	—	.35	2001P	—	.35
1988S *proof only*	—	2.50	2001D	—	.35
1989P	—	.35	2001S *proof only*	—	3.00
1989D	—	.35	2001S Silver, *proof only*	—	5.50
1989S *proof only*	—	3.00	2002P	—	.35
1990P	—	.35	2002D	—	.35
1990D	—	.35	2002S *proof only*	—	2.00
1990S *proof only*	—	2.75	2002S Silver, *proof only*	—	5.00

	XF	BU
2003P	—	.35
2003D	—	.35
2003S *proof only*	—	2.00
2003S Silver, *proof only*	—	5.00
2004P	—	.35
2004D	—	.35
2004S *proof only*	—	2.00
2004S Silver, *proof only*	—	5.00

	XF	BU
2005P	—	.50
2005D	—	.50
2005S *proof only*	—	1.75
2005S Silver, *proof only*	—	3.00
2006P	—	.50
2006D	—	.50
2006S *proof only*	—	2.25
2006S Silver, *proof only*	—	3.00

TWENTY-CENT PIECES

It is evident that even before its release the mint was concerned about the public confusing this coin with a quarter. This is indicated by several features distinct from the other silver coins of the day. The reverse design is a mirror image of that on the others, the word LIBERTY on the shield is in relief rather than incuse, and the edge is plain, not reeded. Nevertheless the public was still confused, and the coin was terminated after only two years in circulation, the 1877 and 1878 dates being collectors' issues.

Known Counterfeits: 1876CC with added mint mark. Some 19th century charlatans would hand-scrape reeding into the edge of pieces in hopes of passing them off as quarters.

1876 Twenty-Cent Piece

	VG	VF
1875	100.00	190.00
1875CC	120.00	225.00
1875S	90.00	130.00
1876	150.00	300.00

	VG	VF
1876CC *Extremely Rare MS-65*		148,500.00
1877	—	2,100.00
1878	—	1,800.00

BUST QUARTERS

Due to limited mint capacity quarters were not struck until 1796, when a small quantity was produced, even though other denominations of United States silver began to be struck two years earlier. These first rare pieces were struck on blanks with crude edges, and often exhibiting "adjustment marks" from filing off of excess silver before striking. The initial reverse design showing a rather skinny eagle within a wreath had been in use only one year when the striking of quarters was suspended. When striking was resumed a few years later it was replaced with a plumper eagle carrying a heraldic shield. Coinage ceased again until 1815 when a cap was added to Liberty and her bust was turned to the left. In the same year a denomination first appeared, not as "quarter dollar" however but "25C."

Rare die combinations of early specimens command a premium from specialists. Cleaning plagues this series, and such pieces are discounted.

Known Counterfeits: Cast counterfeits exist of 1796. Other counterfeits to 1807 are possible.

1796 Quarter with Draped Bust and Small Eagle

DRAPED BUST/SMALL EAGLE

	VG	VF
1796	8,500.00	19,500.00

1804 Quarter with Draped Bust and Heraldic Eagle

DRAPED BUST/HERALDIC EAGLE

	VG	VF		VG	VF
1804	2,500.00	5,500.00	1806	275.00	900.00
1805	275.00	950.00	1807	275.00	925.00
1806, 6 over 5	375.00	1,300.00			

1815 Quarter with Capped Bust

CAPPED BUST TYPE

	VG	VF		VG	VF
1815	70.00	375.00	1824, 4 over 2	130.00	650.00
1818 8 over 5	70.00	450.00	1825, 5 over 2	100.00	500.00
1818	65.00	385.00	1825, 5 over 3	65.00	400.00
1819	75.00	365.00	1825, 5 over 4	65.00	400.00
1820	65.00	365.00	1827		39,600.00
1821	65.00	365.00	1827 proof restrike		47,000.00
1822 25 over 50c	3,000.00	6,750.00	1828	65.00	375.00
1822	90.00	450.00	1828 25 over 50c	300.00	1,000.00
1823, 3 over 2	14,000.00	30,000.00			

1833 Quarter with Capped Bust and No Motto (Reduced Size)

NO MOTTO, REDUCED SIZE

	VG	VF		VG	VF
1831 small letters	65.00	120.00	1835	65.00	120.00
1831 large letters	65.00	120.00	1836	65.00	120.00
1832	65.00	120.00	1837	65.00	120.00
1833	65.00	120.00	1838	65.00	120.00
1834	65.00	120.00			

SEATED LIBERTY QUARTERS

Following the introduction of the Seated Liberty design by Christian Gobrecht on the silver dollar, the smaller coins were gradually brought into harmony with this design. It is generally accepted that the seated goddess version of Liberty was directly or indirectly inspired by depictions of the Roman allegory of Britannia on British coins. The eagle on the reverse is not significantly different from that on the last capped bust coins.

There were several minor changes over the life of this coin. After the first few years, additional drapery was added below Liberty's elbow. The arrows by the date from 1853 to 1855, and the rays on the reverse in 1853 indicate a 7 percent reduction in weight, arrows in 1873 to 1874 a minuscule increase. A ribbon with the motto "In God We Trust" was added over the eagle in 1866.

Known Counterfeits: Genuine 1858 quarters have been re-engraved to pass as 1853 no arrows pieces. Contemporary counterfeits struck in copper, lead, and white metal (tin and lead alloys) exist.

1847 Seated Liberty Quarter with No Motto Above Eagle

NO MOTTO ABOVE EAGLE

	VG	VF		VG	VF
1838	27.00	65.00	1844O	27.00	60.00
1839	28.00	65.00	1845	27.00	45.00
1840O	27.00	110.00	1846	27.00	50.00
1840 extra drapery from elbow	55.00	125.00	1847	27.00	45.00
1840O extra drapery from elbow	50.00	120.00	1847O	40.00	120.00
			1848	55.00	185.00
1841	90.00	185.00	1849	27.00	65.00
1841O	30.00	100.00	1849O	600.00	1,700.00
1842	120.00	275.00	1850	45.00	110.00
1842O small date	650.00	1,850.00	1850O	30.00	100.00
1842O large date	27.00	45.00	1851	75.00	225.00
1843	27.00	45.00	1851O	265.00	575.00
1843O	28.00	100.00	1852	60.00	185.00
1844	27.00	45.00	1852O	250.00	595.00
			1853 no arrows	475.00	900.00

1853O Seated Liberty Quarter with Arrows at Date and Rays on Reverse

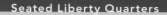

ARROWS AT DATE

	VG	VF
1853	27.00	45.00
1853, 3 over 4	65.50	200.00
1853O	35.00	100.00
1854	27.00	45.00
1854O	27.00	60.00

	VG	VF
1854O huge O	150.00	285.00
1855	27.00	45.00
1855O	60.00	240.00
1855S	60.00	225.00

1856 Seated Liberty Quarter with Arrows Removed From Date

ARROWS REMOVED

	VG	VF
1856	27.00	45.00
1856O	30.00	60.00
1856S	65.00	250.00
1856S, S over S	100.00	375.00
1857	27.00	45.00
1857O	27.00	45.00
1857S	145.00	400.00
1858	27.00	45.00
1858O	30.00	70.00
1858S	100.00	275.00
1859	27.00	45.00
1859O	30.00	80.00

	VG	VF
1859S	135.00	450.00
1860	27.00	45.00
1860O	30.00	55.00
1860S	325.00	900.00
1861	27.00	45.00
1861S	125.00	400.00
1862	27.00	45.00
1862S	125.00	300.00
1863	45.00	120.00
1864	100.00	200.00
1864S	500.00	1,250.00
1865	100.00	200.00
1865S	135.00	350.00

1873 Seated Liberty Quarter, Open 3, with Motto Above Eagle

MOTTO ABOVE EAGLE

	VG	VF		VG	VF
1866	575.00	950.00	1871	60.00	125.00
1866S	325.00	900.00	1871CC	3,800.00	9,500.00
1867	300.00	625.00	1871S	400.00	800.00
1867S	350.00	900.00	1872	40.00	110.00
1868	225.00	400.00	1872CC	850.00	2,950.00
1868S	100.00	300.00	1872S	1,250.00	2,000.00
1869	425.00	675.00	1873 closed 3	225.00	525.00
1869S	125.00	375.00	1873 open 3	42.50	120.00
1870	80.00	200.00	1873CC		four known
1870CC	5,000.00	12,000.00			

1874S Seated Liberty Quarter with Arrows at Date

ARROWS AT DATE

	VG	VF		VG	VF
1873	27.00	60.00	1874	27.00	70.00
1873CC	3,500.00	8,500.00	1874S	30.00	110.00
1873S	40.00	140.00			

1879 Seated Liberty Quarter with Arrows Removed From Date

ARROWS REMOVED

	VG	VF
1875	27.00	45.00
1875CC	90.00	300.00
1875S	36.00	110.00
1876	27.00	45.00
1876CC	27.00	45.00
1876S	27.00	45.00
1877	27.00	45.00
1877CC	28.00	45.00
1877S	27.00	45.00
1877S over		
horizontal S	48.00	125.00
1878	27.00	45.00
1878CC	29.00	85.00
1878S	185.00	350.00
1879	235.00	325.00

	VG	VF
1880	235.00	325.00
1881	250.00	350.00
1882	250.00	350.00
1883	265.00	365.00
1884	400.00	600.00
1885	265.00	365.00
1886	650.00	800.00
1887	350.00	485.00
1888	300.00	420.00
1888S	27.00	45.00
1889	285.00	385.00
1890	85.00	125.00
1891	27.00	45.00
1891O	225.00	550.00
1891S	27.00	65.00

BARBER QUARTERS

The quarter, dime, and half dollar introduced in 1892 bear a portrait head of Liberty instead of an entire figure. They were designed by Chief Engraver Charles E. Barber, after whom they have been popularly named. More practical than artistically adventurous, contemporaries thought the design rather boring if not unpleasant. The reverse of the quarter and the half have a fully spread heraldic eagle, a ribbon in its beak, with a field of stars above. Barber quarters are very common and well worn examples are often regarded as little better than bullion.

Known Counterfeits: 1913S suspected but not confirmed. Contemporary counterfeits in a tin-lead alloy are not rare.

1892 Barber Quarter

	F	XF		F	XF
1892	22.00	70.00	1898O	65.00	235.00
1892O	35.00	82.00	1898S	42.00	75.00
1892S	75.00	150.00	1899	22.00	70.00
1893	25.00	67.00	1899O	30.00	96.00
1893O	27.00	82.00	1899S	70.00	125.00
1893S	50.00	130.00	1900	21.00	70.00
1894	30.00	90.00	1900O	62.00	125.00
1894O	36.00	90.00	1900S	38.00	75.00
1894S	36.00	90.00	1901	228.00	72.00
1895	30.00	75.00	1901O	110.00	365.00
1895O	40.00	110.00	1901S	10,500.00	16,000.00
1895S	45.00	110.00	1902	17.00	65.00
1896	25.00	77.00	1902O	45.00	120.00
1896O	90.00	375.00	1902S	47.00	130.00
1896S	1,250.00	2,950.00	1903	17.00	65.00
1897	21.00	71.00	1903O	38.00	96.00
1897O	80.00	375.00	1903S	45.00	110.00
1897S	220.00	400.00	1904	17.50	65.00
1898	22.00	71.00	1904O	50.00	190.00

1903 Barber Quarter

	F	XF		F	XF
1905	26.00	72.00	1910	25.00	70.00
1905O	80.00	225.00	1910D	40.00	110.00
1905S	40.00	100.00	1911	17.00	72.00
1906	17.00	70.00	1911D	87.00	300.00
1906D	25.00	70.00	1911S	50.00	150.00
1906O	38.00	96.00	1912	17.00	70.00
1907	17.00	65.00	1912S	42.00	110.00
1907D	27.00	80.00	1913	70.00	400.00
1907O	17.00	70.00	1913D	34.00	80.00
1907S	42.00	115.00	1913S	2,850.00	5,300.00
1908	18.00	70.00	1914	17.00	58.00
1908D	17.00	70.00	1914D	17.00	58.00
1908O	17.00	75.00	1914S	165.00	440.00
1908S	75.00	280.00	1915	17.00	65.00
1909	17.00	65.00	1915D	17.00	65.00
1909D	20.00	75.00	1915S	27.00	80.00
1909O	85.00	315.00	1916	17.00	58.00
1909S	30.00	70.00	1916D	17.00	58.00

STANDING LIBERTY QUARTERS

According to many at the time, Hermon MacNeil's Standing Liberty quarter was America's first obscene coin. Many prominent artists thought it an excellent example of inspired neo-classical art. In either case, it was very well debated at the time. Its original version, with a bare breasted Liberty stepping through a gateway while exposing a shield, was ultimately replaced by a more modest one on which she is clad in chain mail. The corrective legislation, however, was careful not to criticize the coin's artistic merit or moral standing openly, thus not offending the Commission of Fine Arts, responsible for its approval. Technically the coin shared with the Buffalo nickel the problem of a high relief date which would wear off. This was partially remedied in 1925 by carving out the area of the date and placing it in the recess. Another technical problem with this quarter was the tendency of Liberty's head to be incompletely struck. As a result high grade pieces with fully struck heads command extra premiums. Examples with the date worn off are worth only their bullion value.

Known Counterfeits: 1916 altered from 1917, 1917 Type I, 1918S 8 over 7, 1923S (altered, including all with round topped 3), 1927S (altered).

1916 Standing Liberty Quarter (Type I)

	F	XF		F	XF
1916	6,750.00	9,500.00	1920S	28.00	55.00
1917	48.00	80.00	1921	290.00	480.00
1917D	48.00	100.00	1923	28.00	40.00
1917S	48.00	145.00	1923S	450.00	750.00
1917	27.00	48.00	1924	20.00	35.00
1917D	65.00	94.00	1924D	95.00	160.00
1917S	62.00	77.00	1924S	38.00	90.00
1918	27.00	45.00	1925	5.00	34.00
1918D	45.00	87.00	1926	5.00	33.00
1918S	32.00	50.00	1926D	15.00	56.00
1918S, 8 over 7	2,500.00	5,900.00	1926S	12.00	100.00
1919	52.00	70.00	1927	5.00	32.00
1919D	165.00	400.00	1927D	19.00	115.00
1919S	160.00	470.00	1927S	65.00	1,000.00
1920	24.00	40.00	1928	5.00	29.00
1920D	75.00	125.00			

1927S Standing Liberty Quarter (Type II)

	F	XF		F	XF
1928D	8.00	38.00	1929S	5.00	30.00
1928S	6.00	32.00	1930	5.00	30.00
1929	5.00	30.00	1930S	6.50	30.00
1929D	6.00	34.00			

WASHINGTON QUARTERS

The Washington quarter was intended to be a one year commemorative for the 200th anniversary of Washington's birth, not a regular issue. Its release was delayed because of the Treasury's decision to change designers from Laura Gardin Fraser to John Flanagan. Both designs were based the 1785 bust of Washington by Houdon. Eventually it was decided to replace the unpopular Standing Liberty quarter with the new commemorative, which enjoyed immense initial popularity.

Several dates in the 1930s are characterized by weak rims making grading difficult. 1934 and 1935 do not have this problem. 1964 pieces were aggressively hoarded in uncirculated rolls, and as such are excessively common.

A special reverse was used in 1975 and 1976 (both with 1976 obverse) to commemorate the American Bicentennial. It depicts the bust of a Colonial drummer designed by Jack L. Ahr.

Known Counterfeits: 1932D and 1932S exist with false mint marks. Counterfeits of high grade 1932 and 1934 pieces also exist.

1936D Washington Quarter

	VF	BU
1932	7.50	24.00
1932D	155.00	1,000.00
1932S	145.00	425.00
1934	3.50	25.00
1934D	10.00	220.00
1935	2.75	21.00
1935D	10.00	220.00
1935S	6.00	85.00
1936	2.75	21.00
1936D	15.00	425.00
1936S	5.50	100.00
1937	3.55	22.00
1937D	5.00	60.00
1937S	11.50	120.00
1938	6.00	70.00
1938S	7.00	70.00
1939	2.50	20.00
1939D	4.50	37.00

	VF	BU
1939S	6.50	75.00
1940	2.50	20.00
1940D	10.00	90.00
1940S	6.00	24.00
1941	2.50	10.00
1941D	3.00	30.00
1941S	2.50	30.00
1942	2.50	7.00
1942D	2.50	17.00
1942S	3.00	75.00
1943	2.50	5.00
1943D	3.50	26.00
1943S	5.00	30.00
1944	2.50	5.00
1944D	2.50	15.00
1944S	2.75	15.00
1945	2.50	5.00
1945D	3.00	17.00

1945 Washington Quarter

1953D Washington Quarter (Silver)

	VF	BU		VF	BU
1945S	2.50	10.00	1953S	1.75	5.00
1946	2.50	5.00	1954	1.50	4.00
1946D	2.50	5.00	1954D	1.50	5.00
1946S	2.50	4.00	1954S	1.50	3.75
1947	2.50	6.00	1955	1.65	3.50
1947D	2.50	4.50	1955D	2.00	4.00
1947S	2.50	4.00	1956	—	4.00
1948	2.50	4.00	1956D	—	3.00
1948D	2.50	9.00	1957	—	3.50
1948S	2.50	6.00	1957D	—	3.00
1949	3.00	30.00	1958	—	3.00
1949D	2.50	20.00	1958D	—	3.00
1950	2.50	6.00	1959	—	3.00
1950D	2.50	5.00	1959D	—	3.00
1950D, D over S	60.00	275.00	1960	—	2.75
1950S	2.50	9.00	1960D	—	2.75
1950S, S over D	65.00	400.00	1961	—	2.75
1951	2.50	6.00	1961D	—	2.75
1951D	2.50	6.00	1962	—	2.75
1951S	3.75	17.00	1962D	—	2.75
1952	2.50	6.00	1963	—	2.75
1952D	2.50	5.00	1963D	—	2.75
1952S	2.50	15.00	1964	—	2.75
1953	2.50	5.00	1964D	—	2.75
1953D	2.50	4.00			

1966 Washington Quarter (Cupro-Nickel Clad Copper)

CUPRO-NICKEL CLAD COPPER

	VF	BU		VF	BU
1965	—	1.00	1972S *proof only*	—	2.00
1966	—	1.00	1973	—	.75
1967	—	1.00	1973D	—	1.00
1968	—	1.00	1973S *proof only*	—	2.00
1968D	—	1.25	1974	—	.75
1968S *proof only*	—	2.50	1974D	—	1.00
1969	—	1.25	1974S *proof only*	—	2.00
1969D	—	1.00	1976 bicentennial	—	1.00
1969S *proof only*	—	2.50	1976D bicentennial	—	1.00
1970	—	1.00	1976S bicentennial,		
1970D	—	1.00	*proof only*	—	2.00
1970S *proof only*	—	2.00	1976S bicentennial,		
1971	—	1.00	Silver Clad	—	3.00
1971D	—	1.00	1977	—	.75
1971S *proof only*	—	2.00	1977D	—	.75
1972	—	.75	1977S *proof only*	—	2.00
1972D	—	.75	1978	—	.75

1976 Washington Quarter with Bicentennial Reverse

	VF	BU
1978D	—	.75
1978S *proof only*	—	2.00
1979	—	.75
1979D	—	.75
1979 thick S, *proof only*	—	2.00
1979 thin S, *proof only*	—	3.00
1980P	—	.75
1980D	—	.75
1980S *proof only*	—	2.00
1981P	—	.75
1981D	—	.75
1981S *proof only*	—	2.00
1982P	—	3.00
1982D	—	1.50
1982S *proof only*	—	3.00
1983P	—	3.00
1983D	—	2.00
1983S *proof only*	—	2.75
1984P	—	1.00
1984D	—	1.25
1984S *proof only*	—	2.75
1985P	—	1.50
1985D	—	2.00
1985S *proof only*	—	1.75
1986P	—	3.00
1986D	—	2.00
1986S *proof only*	—	3.00
1987P	—	.75
1987D	—	.75
1987S *proof only*	—	2.00
1988P	—	1.00
1988D	—	1.00
1988S *proof only*	—	2.25
1989P	—	.75
1989D	—	.75
1989S *proof only*	—	2.25

	VF	BU
1990P	—	.75
1990D	—	.75
1990S *proof only*	—	6.00
1991P	—	.75
1991D	—	.75
1991S *proof only*	—	3.00
1992P	—	.75
1992D	—	.75
1992S *proof only*	—	3.25
1992S Silver, *proof only*	—	4.00
1993P	—	.75
1993D	—	.75
1993S *proof only*	—	3.00
1993S Silver, *proof only*	—	8.55
1994P	—	.75
1994D	—	.75
1994S *proof only*	—	4.00
1994S Silver, *proof only*	—	12.50
1995P	—	.75
1995D	—	.75
1995S *proof only*	—	18.00
1995S Silver, *proof only*	—	18.00
1996P	—	.75
1996D	—	.75
1996S *proof only*	—	4.50
1996S Silver, *proof only*	—	11.50
1997P	—	.75
1997D	—	.75
1997S *proof only*	—	10.00
1997S Silver, *proof only*	—	20.00
1998P	—	.75
1998D	—	.75
1998S *proof only*	—	11.00
1998S Silver, *proof only*	—	10.50

STATE QUARTERS

In 1992, to commemorate its 125th anniversary, Canada released a set of circulating commemorative quarters honoring each province and territory. They were greeted with immense popularity by the general public. Partially inspired by this Canadian series, the United States has begun issuing a similar set of quarters honoring the fifty states. It was the intent of Congress to "promote the diffusion of knowledge among the youth of the United States about the individual states, their history and geography, and the rich diversity of the national heritage."

Five each year will be released from 1999 to 2008. Their release dates will be in the order by which each state ratified the Constitution, with a new quarter appearing roughly every ten weeks. These will be the only quarters issued during these years. None with the eagle reverse will be produced at all.

The designs must meet certain federal criteria, but will be designed and submitted at a state level. Many will be provided by public competitions.

In addition to clad circulation strikes, special silver and clad proof coins will be produced for collectors, much as they have been in previous years.

Known Counterfeits: Apparently risqué designs are actually satirical tokens struck with privately made dies on real quarters.

State Quarter Front

Delaware (1999)

Pennsylvania (1999)

	BU	PF
1999P Delaware	1.50	—
1999D Delaware	1.50	—
1999S Delaware proof only	—	20.00
1999S Delaware Silver, *proof only*	—	40.00

	BU	PF
1999P Pennsylvania	1.50	—
1999D Pennsylvania	1.50	—
1999S Pennsylvania *proof only*	—	15.00
1999S Pennsylvania Silver, *proof only*	—	40.00

New Jersey (1999)

Georgia (1999)

	BU	PF
1999P New Jersey	1.50	—
1999D New Jersey	1.50	—
1999S New Jersey *proof only*	—	15.00
1999S New Jersey Silver, *proof only*	—	40.00

	BU	PF
1999P Georgia	.75	—
1999D Georgia	.75	—
1999S Georgia *proof only*	—	15.00
1999S Georgia Silver, *proof only*	—	40.00

Connecticut (1999)

Massachusetts (2000)

	BU	PF
1999P Connecticut	.75	—
1999D Connecticut	.75	—
1999S Connecticut *proof only*	—	15.00
1999S Connecticut Silver, *proof only*	—	40.00

	BU	PF
2000P Massachusetts	.75	—
2000D Massachusetts	.75	—
2000S Massachusetts *proof only*	—	5.00
2000S Massachusetts Silver, *proof only*	—	10.00

Maryland (2000)

![South Carolina (2000)]

South Carolina (2000)

	BU	PF
2000P Maryland	.75	—
2000D Maryland	.75	—
2000S Maryland *proof only*	—	5.00
2000S Maryland Silver, *proof only*	—	10.00

	BU	PF
2000P South Carolina	.75	—
2000D South Carolina	.75	—
2000S South Carolina *proof only*	—	5.00
2000S South Carolina Silver, *proof only*	—	10.00

New Hampshire (2000)

Virginia (2000)

	BU	PF
2000P New Hampshire	.75	—
2000D New Hampshire	.75	—
2000S New Hampshire		
proof only	—	5.00
2000S New Hampshire		
Silver, *Proof only*	—	10.00

	BU	PF
2000P Virginia	.75	—
2000D Virginia	.75	—
2000S Virginia		
proof only	—	5.00
2000S Virginia Silver,		
proof only	—	10.00

New York (2001)

North Carolina (2001)

	BU	PF
2001P New York	.75	—
2001D NewYork	.75	—
2001S New York		
proof only	—	7.50
2001S New York Silver,		
proof only	—	22.50

	BU	PF
2001P North Carolina	.75	—
2001D North Carolina	.75	—
2001S North Carolina		
proof only	—	7.50
2001S North Carolina		
Silver, *proof only*	—	22.50

Rhode Island (2001)

Vermont (2001)

	BU	PF
2001P Rhode Island	.75	—
2001D Rhode Island	.75	—
2001S Rhode Island *proof only*	—	7.50
2001S Rhode Island Silver, *proof only*	—	22.50

	BU	PF
2001P Vermont	1.00	—
2001D Vermont	.75	—
2001S Vermont *proof only*	—	7.50
2001S Vermont Silver, *proof only*	—	22.50

Kentucky (2001)

Tennessee (2002)

	BU	PF
2001P Kentucky	1.00	—
2001D Kentucky	.75	—
2001S Kentucky *proof only*	—	7.50
2001S Kentucky Silver, *proof only*	—	22.50

	BU	PF
2002P Tennessee	1.00	—
2002D Tennessee	1.00	—
2002S Tennessee *proof only*	—	6.00
2002S Tennessee Silver, *proof only*	—	18.00

Ohio (2002)

Louisiana (2002)

	BU	PF
2002P Ohio	.75	—
2002D Ohio	.75	—
2002S Ohio *proof only*	—	6.00
2002S Ohio Silver, *proof only*	—	18.00

	BU	PF
2002P Louisiana	.75	—
2002D Louisiana	.75	—
2002S Louisiana *proof only*	—	6.00
2002S Louisiana Silver, *proof only*	—	18.00

Indiana (2002)

Mississippi (2002)

	BU	PF
2002P Indiana	.75	—
2002D Indiana	.75	—
2002S Indiana *proof only*	—	6.00
2002S Indiana Silver, *proof only*	—	18.00

	BU	PF
2002P Mississippi	.75	—
2002D Mississippi	.75	—
2002S Mississippi *proof only*	—	6.00
2002S Mississippi Silver, *proof only*	—	18.00

Illinois (2003)

	BU	PF
2003P Illinois	.75	—
2003D Illinois	.75	—
2003S Illinois		
proof only	—	6.00
2003S Illinois Silver,		
proof only	—	10.00

Alabama (2003)

	BU	PF
2003P Alabama	.75	—
2003D Alabama	.75	—
2003S Alabama		
proof only	—	6.00
2003S Alabama Silver,		
proof only	—	10.00

Maine (2003)

	BU	PF
2003P Maine	.75	—
2003D Maine	.75	—
2003S Maine		
proof only	—	6.00
2003S Maine Silver,		
proof only	—	10.00

Missouri (2003)

	BU	PF
2003P Missouri	.75	—
2003D Missouri	.75	—
2003S Missouri		
proof only	—	6.00
2003S Missouri Silver,		
proof only	—	10.00

Arkansas (2003)

	BU	PF
2003P Arkansas	.75	—
2003D Arkansas	.75	—
2003S Arkansas proof only	—	6.00
2003S Arkansas Silver, proof only	—	10.00

Michigan (2004)

	BU	PF
2004P Michigan	.75	—
2004D Michigan	.75	—
2004S Michigan proof only	—	6.00
2004S Michigan Silver, proof only	—	10.00

Florida (2004)

	BU	PF
2004P Florida	.75	—
2004D Florida	.75	—
2004S Florida proof only	—	6.00
2004S Florida Silver, proof only	—	10.00

Texas (2004)

	BU	PF
2004P Texas	.75	—
2004D Texas	.75	—
2004S Texas proof only	—	6.00
2004S Texas Silver, proof only	—	15.00

Iowa (2004)

Wisconsin (2004)

	BU	PF
2004P Iowa	.75	—
2004D Iowa	.75	—
2004S Iowa *proof only*	—	6.00
2004S Iowa Silver, *proof only*	—	10.00

	BU	PF
2004P Wisconsin	.75	—
2004D Wisconsin (3 varieties)	.75	—
2004S Wisconsin *proof only*	—	6.00
2004S Wisconsin Silver, *proof only*	—	10.00

California (2005)

Minnesota (2005)

	BU	PF
2005P California	.75	—
2005D California	.75	—
2005S California *proof only*	—	5.00
2005S California Silver, *proof only*	—	8.00

	BU	PF
2005P Minnesota	.75	—
2005D Minnesota	.75	—
2005S Minnesota *proof only*	—	5.00
2005S Minnesota Silver, *proof only*	—	8.00

Oregon (2005)

Kansas (2005)

	BU	PF
2005P Oregon	.75	—
2005D Oregon	.75	—
2005S Oregon		
proof only	—	5.00
2005S Oregon Silver,		
proof only	—	8.00

	BU	PF
2005P Kansas	.75	—
2005D Kansas	.75	—
2005S Kansas		
proof only	—	5.00
2005S Kansas Silver		
proof only	—	8.00

West Virginia (2005)

	BU	PF
2005P West Virginia	.75	—
2005D West Virginia	.75	—
2005S West Virginia		
proof only	—	5.00
2005S West Virginia		
Silver, proof only	—	8.00

EARLY HALF DOLLARS

The half dollar, along with the half dime and dollar, was one of the first silver denominations to be released by the new United States Mint. As a result, it first appeared with the briefly used flowing hair design. These first rare pieces were struck on blanks with crude edges and often exhibit "adjustment marks" from filing off excess silver before striking. The initial reverse design showing a rather skinny eagle within a wreath continued to be used after the flowing hair obverse was replaced by the rather voluptuous draped bust design. After a brief gap in the issue of halves, this eagle was replaced with a plumper eagle carrying a heraldic shield. In 1807, a cap was added to Liberty's head and her bust was turned to the left. In the same year a denomination first appeared, not as "half dollar" but "50C." The eagle was also made slightly more realistic, though it still bore a heraldic shield. With the introduction of this type, production began to increase. By the teens and twenties halves became so common that banks began to use them as cash reserves to back up their own privately issued paper money. As a result, many half dollars between 1807 and 1839 can be found very well preserved. Unfortunately their high relief caused many of them to be incompletely struck, particularly at the motto over the eagle, and the broach. In 1836, new machinery was introduced and the edges were changed from lettered to reeded.

Rare die combinations of early specimens command a premium from specialists. Cleaning plagues this series, and such pieces are discounted.

Known Counterfeits: Cast counterfeits exist of 1796. Other counterfeits of 1794 to 1802 are possible. Contemporary counterfeits of capped bust halves exist for most dates. They have been struck or cast in brass, copper, tin-lead alloys and German silver. Holed coins are sometimes deceptively plugged.

1795 Half Dollar with Flowing Hair

FLOWING HAIR TYPE

	VG	VF		VG	VF
1794	4,000.00	13,000.00	1795 three leaves . .	1,800.00	6,000.00
1795 two leaves	900.00	3,500.00			

1797 Half Dollar with Draped Bust and Small Eagle

DRAPED BUST/SMALL EAGLE

	VG	VF		VG	VF
1796, 15 stars	30,000.00	55,000.00	1797	30,000.00	55,000.00
1796, 16 stars	36,000.00	60,000.00			

1807 Half Dollar with Draped Bust and Heraldic Eagle

DRAPED BUST/HERALDIC EAGLE

	VG	VF
1801	300.00	1,500.00
1802	300.00	1,500.00
1803 small 3	170.00	600.00
1803 large 3	150.00	500.00
1805, 5 over 4	300.00	990.00
1805	150.00	550.00
1806, 6 over 5	160.00	500.00
1806	130.00	340.00
Note: many varieties of 1806 exist.		
1807	150.00	340.00

1836 Half Dollar with Capped Bust and Lettered Edge

CAPPED BUST/LETTERED EDGE

	VG	VF
1807 small stars	100.00	475.00
1807 large stars	100.00	400.00
1807, 50 over 20	95.00	250.00
1808, 8 over 7	62.00	160.00
1808	60.00	100.00
1809	60.00	100.00
1810	60.00	100.00
1811, 11 over 10	60.00	125.00
1811	60.00	95.00
1812, 2 over 1, small 8	60.00	160.00
1812, 2 over 1, large 8	1,900.00	4,800.00
1812	60.00	100.00
1813	60.00	100.00
1813, 50 C over inverted UNI	63.00	135.00
1814, 4 over 3	70.00	150.00
1814	60.00	100.00
1815, 5 over 2	1,100.00	1,850.00
1817, 7 over 3	125.00	385.00
1817, 7 over 4	60,000.00	145,000.00
1817	60.00	90.00
1818, 8 over 7	70.00	100.00
1818	60.00	85.00
1819, 9 over 8	62.00	100.00
1819	60.00	85.00
1820, 20 over 19	75.00	150.00
1820	60.00	125.00
1821	60.00	80.00
1822, 2 over 1	65.00	150.00
1822	60.00	85.00
1823	62.00	110.00
1824, 4 over 1	60.00	85.00
1824, 4 over 4	60.00	85.00
1824	58.00	75.00
1825	58.00	75.00
1826	58.00	75.00
1827, 7 over 6	65.00	90.00
1827	58.00	75.00
1828	58.00	75.00

Note: date varieties of 1828 exist.

	VG	VF
1829, 9 over 7	58.00	85.00
1829	58.00	70.00
1830	58.00	70.00
1831	58.00	70.00
1832	58.00	70.00
1833	58.00	70.00
1834	58.00	70.00
1835	58.00	70.00
1836	58.00	70.00
1836, 50 over 00	80.00	185.00

1836 Half Dollar with Capped Bust and Reeded Edge

CAPPED BUST/REEDED EDGE

	VG	VF		VG	VF
1836 50 cents	950.00	1,500.00	1838O *proof only*		125,000.00
1837 50 cents	60.00	120.00	1839 half dol	66.00	120.00
1838 half dol	60.00	120.00	1839O half dol	200.00	400.00

SEATED LIBERTY HALF DOLLARS

Following the introduction of the Seated Liberty design by Christian Gobrecht on the silver dollar, the smaller coins were gradually brought into harmony with this design. The half dollar was the last to make the change. It is generally accepted that the seated goddess version of Liberty was directly or indirectly inspired by depictions of the Roman allegory of Britannia on British coins. The eagle on the reverse is not significantly different from that on the last capped bust coins.

There were several minor changes over the life of this coin. During its first year additional drapery was added below Liberty's elbow. The arrows by the date from 1853 to 1855, and the rays on the reverse in 1853 indicate a 7-percent reduction in weight, arrows in 1873 to 1874 a minuscule increase. Most of the 1861O pieces were struck after Louisiana seceded from the Union. A ribbon with the motto "In God We Trust" was added over the eagle in 1866. Seated halves are often found cleaned. Be careful of retoned specimens.

Known Counterfeits: Genuine 1858O halves have been re-engraved to pass as 1853O no arrows pieces. Some with arrows pieces have had the arrows removed for the same reason. Contemporary counterfeits struck in tin and lead alloys are often found.

1839 Seated Liberty Half Dollar with No Motto
Above Eagle and No Drapery Below Elbow

NO MOTTO ABOVE EAGLE

	VG	VF
1839 no drapery below elbow	65.00	315.00
1839 with drapery	35.00	75.00
1840 sm. rev. letters	35.00	70.00
1840 med. rev. letters (struck at New Orleans with 1838 reverse die)	175.00	325.00
1840O	35.00	80.00
1841	50.00	130.00
1841O	35.00	85.00
1842 small date	42.00	110.00
1842 large date	35.00	70.00
1842O small date	850.00	2,250.00
1842O large date	35.00	115.00
1843	35.00	70.00
1843O	35.00	70.00
1844	35.00	70.00
1844O	35.00	70.00
1844O double date	775.00	1,375.00
1845	40.00	110.00
1845O	35.00	70.00
1845O no drapery	35.00	115.00
1846	35.00	70.00
1846, 6 over horizontal 6	235.00	400.00
1846O, med. date	35.00	70.00
1846O, tall date	245.00	575.00
1847, 7 over 6	2,750.00	4,250.00
1847	35.00	70.00
1847O	35.00	70.00
1848	60.00	170.00
1848O	35.00	70.00
1849	40.00	90.00
1849O	35.00	70.00
1850	300.00	500.00
1850O	35.00	80.00
1851	400.00	900.00
1851O	45.00	105.00
1852	500.00	850.00
1852O	125.00	350.00
1853O no arrows	154,000.00	*rare*

1853 Seated Liberty Half Dollar with Arrows at Date and Rays on Reverse

ARROWS AT DATE/
RAYS ON REVERSE

	VG	VF		VG	VF
1853	35.00	90.00	1853O	35.00	125.00

1854 Seated Liberty Half Dollar with Arrows at Date, No Rays on Reverse

ARROWS AT DATE/NO RAYS

	VG	VF		VG	VF
1854	35.00	70.00	1855	35.00	75.00
1854O	35.00	70.00	1855O	35.00	70.00
1855 over 1854	60.00	125.00	1855S	350.00	1,300.00

1858S Seated Liberty Half Dollar with Arrows Removed From Date

ARROWS REMOVED

	VG	VF		VG	VF
1856	35.00	70.00	1860S	35.00	75.00
1856O	35.00	70.00	1861	35.00	70.00
1856S	80.00	260.00	1861O	35.00	70.00
1857	35.00	70.00	1861S	35.00	70.00
1857O	35.00	70.00	1862	40.00	95.00
1857S	115.00	285.00	1862S	35.00	70.00
1858	35.00	70.00	1863	35.00	75.00
1858O	35.00	70.00	1863S	35.00	70.00
1858S	35.00	95.00	1864	35.00	95.00
1859	35.00	70.00	1864S	35.00	70.00
1859O	35.00	70.00	1865	37.00	85.00
1859S	38.00	85.00	1865S	35.00	70.00
1860	35.00	80.00	1866	—	unique
1860O	35.00	70.00	1866S	125.00	375.00

1872CC Seated Liberty Half Dollar with Motto Above Eagle

MOTTO ABOVE EAGLE

	VG	VF
1866	35.00	70.00
1866S	35.00	70.00
1867	35.00	90.00
1867S	35.00	70.00
1868	49.00	135.00
1868S	35.00	70.00
1869	35.00	70.00
1869S	35.00	70.00
1870	35.00	70.00
1870CC	1,200.00	3,000.00
1870S	35.00	70.00

	VG	VF
1871	35.00	70.00
1871CC	325.00	1,200.00
1871S	35.00	70.00
1872	35.00	70.00
1872CC	100.00	325.00
1872S	33.00	110.00
1873 closed 3	35.00	90.00
1873 open 3	2,700.00	5,500.00
1873CC	220.00	800.00
1873S	no known specimens	

1873 Seated Liberty Half Dollar with Arrows at Date

ARROWS AT DATE

	VG	VF
1873	35.00	85.00
1873CC	220.00	725.00
1873S	70.00	225.00

	VG	VF
1874	35.00	85.00
1874CC	550.00	1,500.00
1874S	40.00	160.00

1878S Seated Liberty Half Dollar with Arrows Removed From Date

ARROWS REMOVED

	VG	VF
1875	35.00	70.00
1875CC	35.00	95.00
1875S	35.00	70.00
1876	35.00	70.00
1876CC	35.00	85.00
1876S	35.00	70.00
1877	35.00	70.00
1877CC	33.00	75.00
1877S	35.00	70.00
1878	35.00	70.00
1878CC	525.00	1,250.00
1878S	17,500.00	27,500.00
1879	325.00	425.00
1880	310.00	410.00
1881	300.00	400.00
1882	400.00	500.00
1883	320.00	420.00
1884	425.00	550.00
1885	400.00	500.00
1886	425.00	575.00
1887	500.00	750.00
1888	315.00	400.00
1889	310.00	410.00
1890	310.00	410.00
1891	60.00	120.00

BARBER HALF DOLLARS

The half dollar, quarter, and dime introduced in 1892 bear a portrait of Liberty's head, instead an entire figure. They were designed by Chief Engraver Charles E. Barber, after whom they have been popularly named. Rather practical than artistically adventurous, contemporaries thought the design rather boring, if not unpleasant. The reverse of the half and the quarter have a fully spread heraldic eagle, a ribbon in its beak, with a field of stars above. This new design for the half dollar came only a year following its resurrection as an actively minted denomination. Barbers are very common and well-worn examples are often regarded as little better than bullion. Strong middle grades on the other hand are surprisingly difficult to obtain.

Known Counterfeits: Contemporary counterfeits in a tin-lead alloy are not rare. Altered 1913, 1914, and 1915 coins exist with mint marks removed.

1892 Barber Half Dollar

	VG	VF		VG	VF
1892	38.00	115.00	1895O	30.00	140.00
1892O	300.00	485.00	1895S	46.00	180.00
1892S	300.00	395.00	1896	23.00	130.00
1893	25.00	110.00	1896O	40.00	225.00
1893O	55.00	165.00	1896S	120.00	280.00
1893S	165.00	410.00	1897	12.00	85.00
1894	40.00	130.00	1897O	170.00	750.00
1894O	28.00	125.00	1897S	195.00	475.00
1894S	22.00	100.00	1898	13.00	85.00
1895	19.00	110.00	1898O	60.00	300.00

1903 Barber Half Dollar

1908O Barber Half Dollar

	VG	VF
1898S	39.00	116.00
1899	12.00	85.00
1899O	23.00	120.00
1899S	28.00	110.00
1900	14.00	85.00
1900O	19.00	120.00
1900S	13.00	95.00
1901	12.00	75.00
1901O	20.00	145.00
1901S	39.00	300.00
1902	12.00	75.00
1902O	14.00	95.00
1902S	18.00	115.00
1903	13.00	95.00
1903O	13.00	95.00
1903S	13.00	95.00
1904	12.00	80.00
1904O	23.00	150.00
1904S	52.00	480.00
1905	23.00	130.00
1905O	37.00	200.00
1905S	13.00	100.00
1906	11.00	80.00
1906D	11.00	85.00
1906O	11.00	90.00
1906S	14.00	100.00
1907	11.00	80.00
1907D	11.00	80.00
1907O	11.00	85.00
1907S	18.00	135.00
1908	11.00	80.00
1908D	11.00	80.00
1908O	11.00	80.00
1908S	12.00	100.00
1909	15.00	60.00
1909O	15.00	114.00
1909S	11.00	91.00
1910	20.00	150.00
1910S	13.00	90.00
1911	11.00	70.00
1911D	13.00	85.00
1911S	11.00	84.00
1912	11.00	70.00
1912D	11.00	70.00
1912S	11.00	81.00
1913	45.00	275.00
1913D	13.00	83.00
1913S	11.00	90.00
1914	65.00	395.00
1914S	14.00	81.00
1915	52.00	270.00
1915D	11.00	77.00
1915S	12.00	75.00

WALKING LIBERTY HALF DOLLARS

This artistic new half dollar was designed by Adolph Weinman, the designer of the Mercury dime released in the same year. It depicts Liberty, the American flag draped about her and flowing in the breeze, progressing towards the dawn of a new day. It was received with wide acclaim for its artistic merit when it was first released as part of a program for the beautification of United States coinage. The reverse carries an eagle perched on a rocky crag. The obverse design proved so popular that it was resurrected in 1986 for use on the new silver one ounce bullion coins. Originally the mint marks on this coin appeared on the obverse, but after a matter of months they were moved to the reverse.

Due to the arrangement of the design, Liberty's head does not always strike up fully. High grade examples with fully struck heads are worth more.

Known Counterfeits: 1916S, 1938D coins with added mint mark exist. 1928D halves are all counterfeit.

1921D Walking Liberty Half Dollar

	F	XF		F	XF
1916	70.00	185.00	1917S rev.	16.00	50.00
1916D	60.00	180.00	1918	16.00	150.00
1916S	220.00	580.00	1918D	27.00	185.00
1917	9.00	40.00	1918S	15.00	62.00
1917D obv.	60.00	190.00	1919	60.00	450.00
1917D rev.	34.00	255.00	1919D	67.50	650.00
1917S obv.	90.00	700.00	1919S	43.00	790.00

1944 Walking Liberty Half Dollar

	F	XF
1920	16.00	70.00
1920D	47.50	420.00
1920S	17.00	235.00
1921	275.00	1,500.00
1921D	400.00	2,100.00
1921S	190.00	4,800.00
1923S	24.00	250.00
1927S	13.00	125.00
1928S	14.00	150.00
1929D	13.00	90.00
1929S	12.00	90.00
1933S	12.00	52.00
1934	4.75	9.00
1934D	6.00	29.00
1934S	4.75	27.00
1935	4.75	6.75
1935D	6.00	29.50
1935S	4.75	27.00
1936	4.75	6.00
1936D	4.75	20.00
1936S	4.75	21.00
1937	4.75	8.00
1937D	6.00	29.00
1937S	5.00	23.00
1938	6.00	10.00
1938D	75.00	100.00
1939	4.75	6.00
1939D	4.75	7.50
1939S	6.00	19.00
1940	4.75	6.00
1940S	4.75	8.00
1941	4.75	8.00
1941D	4.75	6.00
1941S	4.75	6.00
1942	4.75	6.00
1942D	4.75	6.00
1942D, D over S	42.00	80.00
1942S	4.75	6.00
1943	4.75	6.00
1943D	4.75	6.00
1943S	4.75	6.00
1944	4.75	6.00
1944D	4.75	6.00
1944S	4.75	6.25
1945	4.75	6.00
1945D	4.75	6.00
1945S	4.75	6.00
1946	4.75	6.00
1946D	6.25	15.00
1946S	4.75	6.25
1947	4.75	9.00
1947D	4.75	10.00

FRANKLIN HALF DOLLARS

Like the design for the Washington Quarter, the design for the Franklin Half Dollar was used in opposition to the recommendation of the Commission of Fine Arts. The reverse depicts the Liberty Bell as its prime motif, despite a law requiring all coins larger than a dime to bear an eagle. This is why a small eagle was added at the side of the bell as an afterthought. While the coin was designed by Chief Engraver John R. Sinnock, the minute eagle was actually engraved by a young Frank Gasparro.

The biggest striking problem of the Franklin Half Dollar is the horizontal lines on the Liberty Bell. Those mint state examples with fully struck bell lines often sell for significantly more.

Known Counterfeits: It is possible that none exist.

1953 Franklin Half Dollar

	XF	MS-60		XF	MS-60
1948	6.50	13.75	1952	5.00	8.00
1948D	5.50	10.00	1952D	5.00	8.00
1949	6.00	45.00	1952S	10.00	38.00
1949D	8.00	35.00	1953	6.00	16.00
1949S	11.00	55.00	1953D	5.00	7.00
1950	6.00	26.00	1953S	6.00	24.00
1950D	7.50	22.00	1954	5.00	7.00
1951	5.00	10.00	1954D	5.00	6.50
1951D	8.00	21.00	1954S	6.00	9.00
1951S	5.00	18.00	1955	19.00	30.00

1962 Franklin Half Dollar

	XF	MS-60
1955 "Bugs Bunny" teeth	—	22.00
1956	5.00	7.00
1957	4.75	6.00
1957D	4.75	5.75
1958	4.75	5.75
1958D	4.75	5.75
1959	4.75	5.75
1959D	4.75	5.75
1960	4.75	5.75
1960D	4.75	5.75
1961	4.75	5.75
1961D	4.75	5.75
1962	4.75	5.75
1962D	4.75	5.75
1963	4.75	5.75
1963D	4.75	5.75

KENNEDY HALF DOLLARS

Only three days had elapsed between the assassination of President John F. Kennedy on November 22, 1963, and the first notice from the director of the mint to the chief engraver to prepare for the issue of a coin bearing his portrait. Gilroy Roberts fashioned its obverse portrait based on the Kennedy inaugural medal to save time. The reverse is Frank Gasparro's rendition of the presidential seal. Remarkably, working dies were ready by January 2. Kennedy halves have been struck in three different compositions. The 1964 issue was struck in the traditional 90-percent silver alloy. The following year when dimes and quarters were changed to cupro-nickel clad copper, the half dollar was preserved as a silver alloy coin by striking it in a silver clad version containing 80-percent silver in its outer layers, and 21-percent silver in its middle layer. The remaining alloy was copper. Finally silver was abandoned in 1971, and only sporadic collectors issues have been struck in that metal since. Circulation issues are now struck in the same clad composition as dimes and quarters. Coins dated 1970D, 1987P and 1987D were not issued to circulation, but are widely available from broken up mint sets.

A special reverse was used in 1975 and 1976 (both with 1976 obverse) to commemorate the American Bicentennial. It depicts Independence Hall in Philadelphia designed by Seth G. Huntington.

Known Counterfeits: It is possible that none exist.

1964 Kennedy Half Dollar with Presidential Seal Reverse

	BU
1964	5.00
1964D	5.50

SILVER CLAD

	BU
1965	2.00
1966	2.00
1967	2.00
1968D	2.00
1968S *proof only*	5.00
1969D	2.00
1969S *proof only*	5.00
1970D	10.00
1970S *proof only*	9.50

CUPRO-NICKEL-CLAD COPPER

	BU
1971	1.55
1971D	1.00
1971S *proof only*	3.00
1972	1.25
1972D	1.25
1972S *proof only*	2.50
1973	1.25
1973D	1.25
1973S *proof only*	2.50
1974	1.25
1974D	1.25
1974S *proof only*	3.00

1976D Kennedy Half Dollar with Bicentennial Reverse

BICENTENNIAL REVERSE

	BU
1976 bicentennial	1.25
1976D bicentennial	1.00
1976S bicentennial *proof only*	1.75
1976S bicentennial Silver Clad	3.50
1977	1.25
1977D	1.25
1977S *proof only*	3.00
1978	1.25
1978D	1.25
1978S *proof only*	2.50
1979	1.25
1979D	1.25
1979 filled S *proof only*	2.50
1979 clear S *proof only*	18.00
1980P	1.25
1980D	1.25
1980S *proof only*	3.00
1981P	1.00
1981D	1.00
1981S *proof only*	3.00
1982P	1.25
1982D	1.25
1982S *proof only*	3.50
1983P	1.25
1983D	1.25
1983S *proof only*	3.50
1984P	1.25
1984D	1.25
1984S *proof only*	5.00
1985P	1.25
1985D	1.25
1985S *proof only*	4.50

	BU
1986P	4.00
1986D	3.00
1986S *proof only*	12.50
1987P	3.00
1987D	3.00
1987S *proof only*	4.00
1988P	1.25
1988D	1.25
1988S *proof only*	8.00
1989P	1.50
1989D	1.50
1989S *proof only*	8.00
1990P	2.00
1990D	2.00
1990S *proof only*	7.00
1991P	1.25
1991D	1.25
1991S *proof only*	14.50
1992P	1.25
1992D	1.25
1992S *proof only*	10.00
1992S Silver, *proof only*	15.00
1993P	1.50
1993D	1.50
1993S *proof only*	14.00
1993S Silver, *proof only*	25.00
1994P	1.50
1994D	1.50
1994S *proof only*	11.00
1994S Silver, *proof only*	35.00
1995P	1.50
1995D	1.50

	BU
1995S *proof only*	47.50
1995S Silver, *proof only*	90.00
1996P	2.00
1996D	2.00
1996S *proof only*	10.00
1996S Silver, *proof only*	50.00
1997P	2.00
1997D	2.00
1997S *proof only*	25.00
1997S Silver, *proof only*	100.00
1998P	2.00
1998D	2.00
1998S *proof only*	18.00
1998S Matte *proof only*	370.00
1998S Silver, *proof only*	30.00
1999P	2.00
1999D	2.00
1999S *proof only*	10.00
1999S Silver, *proof only*	25.00
2000P	2.00
2000D	2.00
2000S *proof only*	7.00
2000S Silver, *proof only*	12.50
2001P	2.00

	BU
2001D	2.00
2001S *proof only*	7.00
2001S Silver, *proof only*	12.50
2002P	3.50
2002D	3.50
2002S *proof only*	8.00
2002S Silver, *proof only*	12.50
2003P	3.00
2003D	3.00
2003S *proof only*	8.00
2003S Silver, *proof only*	12.50
2004P	2.00
2004D	2.00
2004S *proof only*	8.00
2004S Silver, *proof only*	12.50
2005P	2.50
2005D	2.50
2005S *proof only*	7.00
2005S Silver, *proof only*	12.50
2006P	3.00
2006D	3.00
2006S *proof only*	7.00
2006S Silver, *proof only*	12.50

EARLY SILVER DOLLARS

The first American silver dollar was intended to fill the same role in commerce as the old Spanish colonial milled dollar. The dollar, along with the half dollar and half dime, was one of the first silver denominations to be released by the new United States Mint. As a result, it first appeared with the briefly used flowing hair design. These first rare pieces were struck in 1794 and 1795 on crude blanks, often exhibiting "adjustment marks" from the filing off of excess silver before striking.

While considered part of the manufacturing process, these marks nevertheless reduce the value of a specimen. The initial reverse design, showing a rather skinny eagle within a wreath, continued to be used after the flowing hair obverse was replaced by the rather voluptuous draped bust design. After four years of use this eagle was replaced with a plumper eagle carrying a heraldic shield.

As with the smaller denominations, the government's lack of bullion and skilled labor made it impossible to strike enough pieces to have a significant role in the economy. Another complication soon ended the life of the silver dollar altogether. The average silver content of these coins slightly exceeded that of the Spanish dollar, though it was exchangeable for them at par. Most of them were thus exported and melted, worn Spanish dollars being shipped back in their place. Not willing to change the dollar's specifications, the government simply ceased to strike it for thirty years! During the last year they were struck for circulation, 1804, only old dies, probably dated 1803 were used. In the 1830s when a few dollars were needed as gifts for foreign heads of state, the mint struck bust dollars appearing like what the 1804 dollars *would* have looked like if they had borne that date. These exceedingly rare "1804" dollars have become among the most famous United States coins. A small number were also restruck somewhat later for collectors.

Rare die combinations of early coins can command a premium from specialists.

Known Counterfeits: It is likely that all dates of early dollars have been counterfeited. Some of the cruder counterfeits can be easily distinguished by the plain or reeded edges they have, as opposed to the lettered edges of the authentic pieces. Other counterfeits are more dangerous. A false

1794 is known re-engraved from a real 1795 A great many counterfeit 1804s exist. Holed coins are sometimes deceptively plugged. Cleaning is a frequent problem, both on real and counterfeit pieces. On the latter it can sometimes make authentication more difficult.

1795 Silver Dollar with Flowing Hair

FLOWING HAIR TYPE

	VG	VF		VG	VF
1794	30,000.00	80,500.00	1795	19,000.00	5,500.00

1795 Silver Dollar with Draped Bust and Small Eagle

DRAPED BUST/SMALL EAGLE

	VG	VF		VG	VF
1795	1,050.00	3,300.00	1797 10 stars l. & 6 stars r.	1,100.00	3,400.00
1796	1,025.00	3,250.00	1798 15 stars	1,600.00	3,800.00
1797 9 & 7 stars, small letters	2,000.00	5,000.00	1798 13 stars	1,250.00	3,400.00
1797 9 & 7 stars, large letters	1,100.00	3,400.00			

1798 Silver Dollar with Draped Bust and Heraldic Eagle

DRAPED BUST/HERALDIC EAGLE

	VG	VF
1798	800.00	2,000.00
1799 9 over 8, 15 stars	900.00	2,000.00
1799 9 over 8, 13 stars	900.00	2,100.00
1799	800.00	2,000.00
1799 8 stars l. & 5 stars r.	900.00	2,500.00
1800	900.00	2,000.00
1801	950.00	2,200.00
1802 2 over 1	950.00	2,500.00
1802	950.00	2,500.00
1802 *proof restrike*	—	175,000.00
1803	950.00	2,500.00
1803 *proof restrike*	—	135,000.00
1804 (struck 1834-35) *proof*	—	1,815,000.00
1804 (struck 1859) *proof*	—	875,000.00

GOBRECHT DOLLARS

It is ironic that the coin for which the Seated Liberty design was first prepared was the last to have it appear on pieces actively struck for circulation. It was the intent that when the striking of silver dollars was resumed, a design of exceptional artistic merit be used. For this reason, Christian Gobrecht was asked to prepare dies based on a drawing of Liberty seated by artist Thomas Sully. It is generally accepted that his seated goddess concept of Liberty derives from depictions of the Roman allegory of Britannia on British coins. The reverse design was also a radical departure from the staid old heraldic eagle. The new eagle was seen in the realistic attitude of flight. It was prepared by Gobrecht based on a drawing of Old Pete by the famous Titian Peale. Old Pete was an eagle who lived at the mint ca.1830-36 and who met an unfortunate end, getting caught in the machinery. While Gobrecht dollars are not all patterns, very few were ever struck for circulation, never more than a thousand or so of any one variety. Only circulating issues are listed here. Pattern pieces with the engraver's name in the field as opposed to on the base, as well as 1838 issues, are listed in that section. Later, some were restruck for collectors. These can usually be distinguished by the misaligned dies which make the eagle appear to be flying horizontally when the coin is turned around. Originals have the eagle flying slightly upward.

Known Counterfeits: Gobrecht experimental dollars are less often counterfeited than other early dollars. Cleaning and polishing are problems.

1836 Gobrecht Dollar with Stars on Reverse

STARS ON REVERSE

	VF	EF		VF	EF
1836 (coin alignment)	6,500.00	9,000.00	1836 (struck 1837, medal alignment)	6,500.00	9,000.00

1839 Gobrecht Dollar with Stars on Obverse

STARS ON OBVERSE

	VF	EF
1839	10,000.00	15,000.00

SEATED LIBERTY DOLLARS

The active production of silver dollars was finally resumed in 1840. However, the reverse design especially created for them was replaced by a more mundane heraldic eagle, similar to that in use on the minor coinage. While production of these coins continued for most years, those struck from 1853 to about 1867 were primarily intended as bullion pieces for export, each containing more than a dollar's worth of silver. A ribbon with the motto "In God We Trust" was added over the eagle in 1866. These dollars are often found cleaned. Be careful of retoned specimens as well.

Known Counterfeits: Counterfeits of this type are not common.

NO MOTTO ABOVE EAGLE

	F	EF		F	EF
1840	265.00	525.00	1846	265.00	425.00
1841	265.00	425.00	1846O	300.00	1,250.00
1842	265.00	425.00	1847	265.00	425.00
1843	265.00	370.00	1848	425.00	750.00
1844	300.00	500.00	1849	265.00	425.00
1845	285.00	550.00	1850	700.00	1,100.00

1845 Seated Liberty Dollar with No Motto Above Eagle

	F	EF		F	EF
1850O	375.00	1,400.00	1859	265.00	600.00
1851 original	8,000.00	13,500.00	1859O	265.00	425.00
1851 restrike proof	—	21,000.00	1859S	400.00	1,350.00
1852 original	6,500.00	11,500.00	1860	275.00	475.00
1852 restrike proof	—	20,000.00	1860O	265.00	425.00
1853	285.00	600.00	1861	650.00	1,250.00
1854	1,600.00	3,700.00	1862	675.00	1,200.00
1855	1,400.00	3,650.00	1863	450.00	990.00
1856	600.00	975.00	1864	315.00	675.00
1857	550.00	1,100.00	1865	290.00	625.00
1858	3,350.00	5,500.00	1866		*two known*

1871 Seated Liberty Dollar with Motto Above Eagle

MOTTO ABOVE EAGLE

	F	EF		F	EF
1866	285.00	550.00	1869	265.00	440.00
1867	300.00	600.00	1870	265.00	440.00
1868	265.00	525.00	1870CC	500.00	1,450.00

	F	EF
1870S	60,000.00	175,000.00
1871	265.00	425.00
1871CC	3,750.00	8,950.00
1872	265.00	425.00
1872CC	1,750.00	4,250.00

	F	EF
1872S	400.00	1,100.00
1873	265.00	425.00
1873CC	6,500.00	17,500.00
1873S	none known to exist	

TRADE DOLLARS

Trade dollars were coins struck deliberately for export as bullion, usually to the Far East. They were chiefly intended to compete against the Mexican peso which had slightly more silver than a standard dollar. They were distinguished by a Liberty and eagle facing the opposite direction from the standard dollars. From the very beginning their legal tender status was limited in the United States, but in 1876 when the price of silver dropped they ceased to have legal tender altogether, not having it restored until 1965! Eight million were redeemed by the government in 1887. Any struck between 1879 and 1885 are Proof Only collectors' issues. Prices listed for them are for circulated examples.

It was typical for Oriental merchants to impress a character into these and other silver coins, to confirm that they accepted them as good quality. These "chop marks" are commonly found on trade dollars, sometimes in quantity. They reduce the value of the coin as a form of mutilation, but have recently been the subject of serious research. Chop marked dollars may not be as valuable, but are still collectible.

Known Counterfeits: Counterfeits are not abundant and are more likely to be contemporary counterfeits. Be cautious of cleaned coins.

1876 Trade Dollar

	F	EF		F	EF
1873	125.00	250.00	1877	125.00	175.00
1873CC	225.00	700.00	1877CC	210.00	400.00
1873S	160.00	260.00	1877S	125.00	175.00
1874	150.00	240.00	1878 *proof only*	—	1,250.00
1874CC	125.00	240.00	1878CC	675.00	1,750.00
1874S	125.00	175.00	1878S	125.00	175.00
1875	400.00	650.00	1879 *proof only*	—	950.00
1875CC	125.00	200.00	1880 *proof only*	—	950.00
1875S	125.00	175.00	1881 *proof only*	—	1,000.00
1875S, S over CC	400.00	695.00	1882 *proof only*	—	1,000.00
1876	125.00	175.00	1883 *proof only*	—	1,200.00
1876CC	200.00	375.00	1884 *proof only*	—	*ten known*
1876S	125.00	175.00	1885 *proof only*	—	*five known*

MORGAN DOLLARS

The Morgan dollar was introduced as a result of pressure from the silver mining lobby. For decades, silver dollars had been scarce in circulation. With the boom in silver mining, the price of the metal dropped as more became available. Something needed to be done to remove the excess silver from the market. The new design coincided with the reintroduction of the silver dollar. Because they were inconvenient, however, many, perhaps hundreds of thousands, of these dollars sat for decades in bags, held as private, bank, and government reserves. The U.S. Treasury was stuck with such an excess that thousands remained on hand for almost a century, prompting the famous GSA auction of silver dollars in the 1970s. Those coins in distinctive GSA cases often command a slight premium.

Artistically many consider the Morgan dollar, named after its designer, George T. Morgan, an aesthetically pleasing but unoriginal design. Morgan's competence (and perhaps his interesting use of Gothic script) may perhaps be attributed to his training at the Royal Mint in London. A long gap exists between 1904 and the last Morgan issue in 1921. During this time the master dies were lost and new ones had to be prepared. As a result, there are subtle differences of relief in the 1921 issue. It is less pleasing and dealer "bids" are often less for that year than for other bulk Morgan dollars. Another subtle variation in the appearance of Morgan dollars is the variation in quality of strike from mint to mint. San Francisco-made examples are usually fully struck, Philadelphia are medium, and New Orleans dollars are usually the most weakly struck. The eagle's breast on high-grade pieces is usually the spot where these differences are most obvious.

Morgans have been among the most popular coins to invest in. This is partially due to their availability in great quantities in uncirculated condition, the typical grade favored by investment promoters and the mass of investors. It is ironic that their sheer commonness has contributed to their desirability.

Known Counterfeits: Genuine coins have been known altered to pass for 1879CC, 1889CC, 1892S, 1893S, 1894, 1895, 1895S, 1896S, 1901, 1903S and 1904S dates. Cast counterfeits are known of 1878, 1878S, 1879S, 1880O, 1881, 1883, 1883S, 1885, 1888O, 1889, 1889O, 1892O, 1899O, 1901, 1902, 1903, 1904S, 1921D and 1921S. Struck counterfeits of certain rare dates are also possible. Cleaned coins are common and are heavily discounted, as are scuffed and heavily edge-knocked pieces. Be careful to avoid coins with false toning.

1881CC Morgan Dollar

	VF	MS-60
1878, 8 tail feathers	25.00	125.00
1878, 7 over 8 tail feathers	22.00	115.00
1878, 7 feathers	20.00	56.00
1878, 7 feathers, rev. of 1879	19.00	67.00
1878CC	95.00	220.00
1878S	19.50	46.00
1879	18.00	30.00

	VF	MS-60
1879CC	145.00	2,650.00
1879O	18.00	72.00
1879S	18.00	40.00
1880	18.00	30.00
1880CC	115.00	480.00
1880O	18.00	60.00
1880S	18.00	33.00
1881	18.00	30.00
1881CC	300.00	500.00

	VF	MS-60
1881O	18.00	30.00
1881S	18.00	30.00
1882	18.00	30.00
1882CC	95.00	215.00
1882O	18.00	32.50
1882O, O over S	30.00	170.00
1882S	18.00	33.00
1883	18.00	30.00
1883CC	100.00	210.00
1883O	18.00	30.00
1883S	18.00	490.00
1884	18.00	30.00
1884CC	95.00	205.00
1884O	18.00	30.00

	VF	MS-60
1884S	18.50	4,100.00
1885	18.50	30.00
1885CC	375.00	560.00
1885O	18.50	30.00
1885S	27.50	185.00
1886	18.50	30.00
1886O	18.50	505.00
1886S	48.50	240.00
1887, 7 over 6	33.00	250.00
1887	18.00	30.00
1887O, 7 over 6	30.00	350.00
1887O	18.00	54.00
1887S	18.50	100.00
1888	18.50	30.00

1887O Morgan Dollar

	VF	MS-60
1888O	18.00	30.00
1888S	80.00	240.00
1889	18.50	30.00
1889CC	1,700.00	17,500.00
1889O	18.00	140.00
1889S	55.00	200.00
1890	18.00	30.00
1890CC	94.00	350.00
1890O	18.00	56.00
1890S	18.00	56.00
1891	18.00	51.00
1891CC	95.00	345.00
1891O	18.00	135.00
1891S	18.00	60.00
1892	18.50	150.00

	VF	MS-60
1892CC	160.00	825.00
1892O	19.50	100.00
1892S	46.00	34,000.00
1893	140.00	540.00
1893CC	335.00	3,130.00
1893O	230.00	1,500.00
1893S	5,000.00	75,000.00
1894	1,250.00	3,200.00
1894O	57.50	550.00
1894S	68.50	570.00
1895 proof only	—	22,000.00
1895O	340.00	13,000.00
1895S	335.00	2,250.00
1896	18.00	30.00
1896O	18.50	940.00

1892S Morgan Dollar

1901 Morgan Dollar

	VF	MS-60		VF	MS-60
1896S	47.50	1,250.00	1901O	18.00	32.00
1897	18.00	30.00	1901S	29.00	340.00
1897O	18.50	650.00	1902	18.00	42.50
1897S	18.50	56.00	1902O	18.00	30.00
1898	18.50	30.00	1902S	100.00	375.00
1898O	18.50	30.00	1903	50.00	67.50
1898S	22.50	260.00	1903O	250.00	400.00
1899	54.00	125.00	1903S	100.00	3,800.00
1899O	18.50	30.00	1904	20.00	80.00
1899S	25.00	325.00	1904O	20.00	33.00
1900	18.00	30.00	1904S	50.00	990.00
1900O	18.00	32.00	1921	12.50	19.50
1900O, O over CC	34.00	230.00	1921D	12.50	40.00
1900S	19.50	245.00	1921S	12.50	30.00
1901	30.00	1,800.00			

PEACE DOLLARS

Like the Morgan dollar before it, the Peace dollar was the result of Congressional authorization for a new large coinage of silver dollars. When the famous numismatist Farran Zerbe learned that this new issue of dollars was to bear the old Morgan design he agitated for a new, artistically more progressive replacement. This was to be a new radiant Liberty head by sculptor Anthony de Francisci. It was not only in harmony with the new designs for the other denominations, especially those by Weinman and St. Gaudens, but also commemorated the end of World War I. The word PEACE can be seen upon the rocky perch on which the eagle stands. The very first Peace Dollars, those struck in 1921 only, were struck in a much higher relief. Later issues have a lower relief more suitable to mass production. The old silver dollar was last made for circulation in 1935. The Peace dollar out-lived this death sentence for thirty years in the form of the mysterious issue of 1964. While none have been officially verified, there have long been rumors, generally accepted by the numismatic community, that several escaped the mint's melting pot.

Like the Morgan dollar, this coin is available in mint state in abundant quantities. The broad smooth surfaces, however, permit many mint state pieces to reveal unsightly bruises and bag marks.

Known Counterfeits: 1928 altered from 1923 or 1928S, as well as other counterfeits of this date.

1921 Peace Dollar

	VF	MS-60
1921	92.00	210.00
1922	12.00	16.00
1922D	12.00	24.00
1922S	12.00	23.00
1923	12.00	16.00
1923D	12.00	53.00
1923S	12.00	28.00
1924	12.00	16.00
1924S	31.00	195.00
1925	12.00	16.00
1925S	20.00	75.00
1926	15.00	34.00
1926D	15.00	60.00

	VF	MS-60
1926S	14.00	40.00
1927	31.50	70.00
1927D	21.50	145.00
1927S	28.50	135.00
1928	425.00	500.00
1928S	32.50	140.00
1934	21.50	105.00
1934D	19.50	110.00
1934S	45.00	1,700.00
1935	21.50	62.00
1935S	16.50	250.00
1964D	*no confirmed examples known*	

EISENHOWER DOLLARS

The "Ike" dollar was struck as much to commemorate the first manned moon landing in 1969, as to honor President Dwight D. Eisenhower. The reverse of this coin was an adaptation of the Apollo XI insignia, depicting an eagle clutching an olive branch and landing on the moon. The obverse shows a left-facing portrait of Eisenhower. Circulation strikes were of the same cupro-nickel clad composition as the dime and quarter. Special collectors' issues were also struck in a silver clad version similar to the alloy used for the half dollars of 1965-1970. These special silver coins bearing the "S" mint mark were released in blue envelopes for the uncirculated issues, and brown boxes for the proofs. Most dealers and collectors require that they be in the original packaging.

A special reverse was used to commemorate the bicentennial. It featured the Liberty Bell superimposed on the moon, as arranged by design contest winner Dennis R. Williams. While all bicentennial dollars are dated "1776-1976," they were struck in both 1975 and 1976. The reverse of the former year uses heavy block lettering, the latter mostly used slightly finer letters. They are easily identified by the lack of copper on the reeded edge.

Known Counterfeits: Poor quality counterfeits have recently come out of Communist China. Specifically 1976D is known.

1974D Eisenhower Dollar with Eagle Reverse

	MS-63	PF
1971	—	3.75
1971D	—	2.25
1971S Silver	6.00	7.00
1972	—	2.75
1972D	—	2.25
1972S Silver	6.50	7.00
1973	—	11.00

	MS-63	PF
1973D	—	11.00
1973S proof only	—	11.00
1973S Silver	8.50	30.00
1974	—	3.00
1974D	—	2.75
1974S proof only	—	6.50
1974S Silver	7.50	7.25

1976D Eisenhower Dollar with Bicentennial on Reverse

BICENTENNIAL REVERSE

	MS-63	PF
1976 block letters	—	6.00
1976 finer letters	—	2.00
1976D block letters	—	3.25
1976D finer letters	—	2.00
1976S block letters proof only	—	6.00
1976S finer letters proof only	—	6.00
1976S Silver, block letters	14.00	13.00

REGULAR ISSUE CONTINUED

	MS-63	PF
1977	—	4.25
1977D	—	3.25
1977S proof only	—	8.00
1978	—	2.75
1978D	—	3.00
1978S proof only	—	10.00

SUSAN B. ANTHONY DOLLARS

The Anthony "mini-dollar" was struck to achieve two specific ends. It was intended to save the government money, by replacing the quickly worn out one dollar bill with a coin which would last in circulation for decades. It was also a coin greatly supported and pushed for by the vending machine lobby. The large Ike dollars were inconvenient for vending machines, but a coin of its value was necessary to facilitate the sale of more expensive items in such machines.

Its obverse depicts Frank Gasparro's portrait of Susan B. Anthony who was instrumental in gaining women the right to vote. The reverse design is the same Apollo XI motif as on the Eisenhower dollar.

Certainly one of the least popular coins in the history of the United States, it was far too close in diameter to the quarter, with which it was frequently confused. It was of the same clad composition. The third year of issue was not even placed into circulation, and was just obtainable in mint sets. The final year was only struck in anticipation of its immediate replacement by the Sacagawea dollar.

Known Counterfeits: Not common.

1979S Susan B. Anthony with Filled S Mark

	MS-63	PF
1979P narrow rim, far date	—	2.00
1979P wide rim, near date	—	12.00
1979D	—	1.75
1979S	—	2.00
1979S filled S	—	8.00
1979S clear S	—	100.00
1980	—	2.00

	MS-63	PF
1980D	—	2.00
1980S	2.00	8.00
1981	—	6.00
1981D	—	6.00
1981S	—	6.00
1981S filled S	—	8.00
1981S clear S	—	220.00
1999P	1.75	9.50
1999D	—	1.75

SACAGAWEA DOLLARS

Despite the failure of the SBA to win any amount of popular acceptance at all, the reasons why it was originally issued remained. The government could save millions by replacing the dollar bill with a more durable coin. Also a dollar coin of moderate size was still sought by the vending machine industry to facilitate the sale of more expensive items.

The confusion caused by the Anthony dollar was eliminated by changing the color, and giving the new coin a broad border. This new, well-designed coin depicts Sacagawea, the Shoshone Indian guide and translator who accompanied the Lewis and Clark Expedition to explore the Northwest (1804-06). She carries her infant son on her back. It is the work of Glenna Goodacre. The reverse, designed by Thomas D. Rogers, Jr., depicts a graceful eagle in flight.

While it is the same size as the Anthony dollar, it has a unique composition. It is a brass of 77% copper, 12% zinc, 7% manganese, and 4% nickel, bonded to a pure copper core. This coin is prone to spotting. Mint state examples lacking spots are more desirable.

Known Counterfeits: Quantities are known, primarily made for circulation in Ecuador.

2002D Sacagawea Dollar

	MS-63	PF		MS-63	PF
2000P	—	2.00	2001S	—	80.00
2000D	—	2.00	2002P	—	2.00
2000S	—	10.00	2002D	—	2.00
2001P	—	4.00	2002S	—	26.00
2001D	—	4.00	2003P	—	2.50

	MS-63	PF		MS-63	PF
2003D	—	2.50	2005D	—	2.50
2003S	—	16.00	2005S	—	15.00
2004P	—	2.50	2006P	—	2.50
2004D	—	2.50	2006D	—	2.50
2004S	—	16.00	2006S	—	16.00
2005P	—	2.50			

1 Dollar Gold Pieces

Although the gold dollar was originally planned as early as 1791, and patterns were prepared in 1836, it was not until 1849 that they were finally approved. Earlier demand was being filled by privately struck Georgia and Carolina gold of standard United States coinage weight, and the mint director personally opposed their issue. When Congressional intervention was coupled with the new flow of gold from California, the mint had to give in. The first gold dollars, designed as one of James Longacre's early projects, were a mere 12.7 mm. in diameter and were easily lost. The diameter was increased to 14.3 mm. and the coin made thinner in 1854 to make them easier to handle, but the new narrow head design was of too high relief and parts of the date on the reverse did not always strike up. The gold dollar's final modification came in 1856, when the wide flan was retained but a lower-relief portrait of Liberty similar to that on the Three Dollar piece was used.

Many gold dollars were used at the time in jewelry and bear solder marks, especially the first type. These coins are worth a fraction of the value of unmutilated coins. Mutilated examples are far more common than worn ones, with few examples grading lower than VF.

Known Counterfeits: 1849C open wreath and 1854C exist, made by altering genuine coins of other dates or mints. Cast counterfeits have been made of 1850-54. It is important to note that struck counterfeits exist of virtually every date in this series.

1849 Dollar Gold Piece with Coronet - Type I

CORONET HEAD—TYPE I

	VF	EF
1849 open wreath	140.00	190.00
1849 closed wreath	135.00	185.00
1849C open wreath	*extremely rare*	
1849C closed wreath	950.00	1,250.00
1849D	1,150.00	1,600.00
1849O	150.00	230.00
1850	135.00	190.00
1850C	995.00	1,300.00
1850D	1,150.00	1,600.00
1850O	240.00	350.00
1851	135.00	190.00
1851C	995.00	1,300.00
1851D	1,150.00	1,600.00
1851O	160.00	200.00
1852	135.00	190.00
1852C	995.00	1,300.00
1852D	1,150.00	1,600.00
1852O	140.00	230.00
1853	135.00	190.00
1853C	995.00	1,300.00
1853D	1,150.00	1,600.00
1853O	160.00	210.00
1854	135.00	190.00
1854D	1,200.00	2,000.00
1854S	290.00	420.00

1854 Dollar Gold Piece with Narrow Indian Princess Head - Type II

NARROW INDIAN PRINCESS HEAD—TYPE II

	VF	EF
1854	280.00	415.00
1855	280.00	415.00
1855C	1,200.00	3,000.00
1855D	4,250.00	8,250.00
1855O	425.00	600.00
1856S	725.00	1,200.00

1860D Dollar Gold Piece with Large Indian Princess Head - Type III

LARGE INDIAN PRINCESS HEAD—
TYPE III

	VF	EF		VF	EF
1856 upright 5	145.00	195.00	1867	400.00	490.00
1856 slanted 5	140.00	190.00	1868	275.00	400.00
1856D	3,400.00	5,400.00	1869	335.00	520.00
1857	140.00	190.00	1870	275.00	390.00
1857C	950.00	1,400.00	1870S	445.00	725.00
1857D	1,150.00	1,750.00	1871	275.00	370.00
1857S	500.00	600.00	1872	275.00	350.00
1858	140.00	190.00	1873 closed 3	400.00	750.00
1858D	1,150.00	1,500.00	1873 open 3	135.00	190.00
1858S	375.00	500.00	1874	135.00	190.00
1859	140.00	190.00	1875	1,850.00	3,650.00
1859C	950.00	1,500.00	1876	275.00	350.00
1859D	1,150.00	1,500.00	1877	175.00	335.00
1859S	225.00	480.00	1878	200.00	350.00
1860	140.00	190.00	1879	180.00	270.00
1860D	2,500.00	3,800.00	1880	160.00	200.00
1860S	325.00	465.00	1881	160.00	200.00
1861	140.00	190.00	1882	170.00	210.00
1861D (Struck by the Confederacy)	6,400.00	9,000.00	1883	160.00	200.00
1862	135.00	190.00	1884	150.00	200.00
1863	425.00	825.00	1885	160.00	200.00
1864	350.00	440.00	1886	160.00	200.00
1865	350.00	550.00	1887	160.00	200.00
1866	360.00	425.00	1888	160.00	200.00
			1889	160.00	200.00

2-1/2 DOLLAR GOLD PIECES

The first strikes of the quarter eagle (gold 2-1/2 dollar piece) came the year following the first introduction of American gold coinage, the half eagle and eagle preceding it in 1795. However, it preceded the other denominations as being the first coin to depict the heraldic eagle bearing a shield on its chest, which later was featured on all denominations other than copper. Its first obverse features a bust of Liberty wearing a tall conical cap, traditionally but inaccurately referred to by numismatists as a turban. This first bust by Robert Scott was replaced by one designed by John Reich, and had a smaller cap. A reverse eagle similar, but more realistic, was paired with the new obverse. A large gap in the striking of quarter eagles followed immediately upon the release of this new design, which was finally restored on the same standard but at a slightly smaller diameter in 1821.

Through most of its history until the 1830s, the quarter eagle was plagued by mass meltings, because it was undervalued relative to its gold content, particularly by European standards. In 1834, this was remedied by reducing the coin's gold content. This was indicated to the public by the removal of the motto over the eagle on the reverse, and by a new capless Liberty head, the "Classic Head" by William Kneass. The final Coronet-type Liberty head design was a rendition by Christian Gobrecht, which continued in use from 1840 to 1907 without change. Those 1848 pieces countermarked CAL. were struck with gold shipped east by the military governor of California.

In 1908, as part of the same coin design beautification program which later introduced the Walking Liberty half dollar and St. Gaudens double eagle, sculptor Bela Lyon Pratt was asked to prepare new designs for the quarter and half eagle in secret under the authority of President Theodore Roosevelt. His work showed the bust of an Indian chief on the obverse and an eagle with closed wings on the reverse. It was both controversial and innovative in that it bore its design in relief, but recessed below the surface of the coin. While some criticized it both for aesthetic reasons and for fear of it spreading germs in dirt trapped in the recesses, it proved to be a very successful method of shielding the design from wear.

Known Counterfeits: Examples of 1848 CAL, 1875, and 1911D exist made by altering genuine coins of other dates or mints. Struck counterfeits exist of virtually every date in this series. All examples of 1905S are counterfeit—no real ones exist. Be cautious of false C mint marks altered by cutting down an authentic O mint mark. Beware of traces of solder on earlier coins from use as jewelry. Look for interruption in the pattern of edge reeding. Be cautious of cleaned coins. This is harder to detect on gold, which usually does not tone naturally.

1807 2-1/2 Dollar Gold Piece with Turban Bust

TURBAN BUST RIGHT

	F	XF		F	XF
1796 no stars on obverse	25,000.00	70,000.00	1804, 13 stars	23,500.00	70,000.00
1796 stars	22,500.00	60,000.00	1804, 14 stars	4,350.00	7,950.00
1797	14,000.00	21,500.00	1805	4,350.00	7,950.00
1798	5,500.00	9,750.00	1806, 6 over 4	4,500.00	8,000.00
1802, 2 over 1	5,000.00	8,600.00	1806, 6 over 5	7,600.00	13,500.00
			1807	4,350.00	7,250.00

1831 2-1/2 Dollar Gold Piece with Capped Bust

CAPPED BUST TYPE

	F	XF
1808	22,500.00	34,000.00
1821	5,000.00	7,500.00
1824, 4 over 1	5,000.00	7,200.00
1825	5,000.00	7,200.00
1826, 6 over 5	5,250.00	8,000.00
1827	5,300.00	8,500.00
1829	4,600.00	6,500.00
1830	4,600.00	6,500.00
1831	4,600.00	6,500.00
1832	4,600.00	6,500.00
1833	4,600.00	6,600.00
1834	7,000.00	15,500.00

1834 2-1/2 Dollar Gold Piece with Classic Head (No Motto)

CLASSIC HEAD (NO MOTTO)

	F	XF
1834	250.00	465.00
1835	250.00	465.00
1836	250.00	465.00
1837	250.00	650.00
1838	250.00	465.00
1838C	850.00	2,000.00
1839	250.00	650.00
1839C	850.00	2,200.00
1839D	850.00	2,800.00
1839O	365.00	925.00

1842O 2-1/2 Dollar Gold Piece with Coronet (No Motto)

CORONET TYPE (NO MOTTO)

	F	EF
1840	150.00	850.00
1840C	825.00	1,600.00
1840D	1,200.00	8,000.00
1840O	225.00	800.00
1841	—	87,500.00
1841C	675.00	1,600.00
1841D	990.00	3,850.00
1842	450.00	2,900.00
1842C	700.00	2,800.00
1842D	900.00	3,350.00
1842O	220.00	1,100.00
1843	150.00	220.00
1843C, crosslet 4, small date	1,100.00	5,000.00
1843C, plain 4, large date	600.00	1,600.00
1843D	700.00	1,850.00
1843O, crosslet 4, small date	150.00	250.00
1843O, plain 4, large date	200.00	450.00
1844	225.00	850.00
1844C	600.00	1,850.00
1844D	650.00	1,850.00
1845	180.00	300.00
1845D	725.00	1,850.00
1845O	525.00	2,000.00
1846	200.00	500.00
1846C	750.00	3,500.00
1846D	700.00	1,850.00

	F	EF
1846O	170.00	400.00
1847	140.00	360.00
1847C	700.00	1,600.00
1847D	700.00	1,850.00
1847O	150.00	375.00
1848	315.00	850.00
1848 CAL.	6,500.00	24,000.00

Quarter eagles with CAL over the eagle were struck with gold shipped to the Dept. of War by the governor of California.

	F	EF
1848C	600.00	1,650.00
1848D	700.00	1,850.00
1849	200.00	475.00
1849C	700.00	1,750.00
1849D	700.00	1,850.00
1850	140.00	215.00
1850C	700.00	1,650.00
1850D	700.00	1,850.00
1850O	160.00	450.00
1851	135.00	200.00
1851C	700.00	1,650.00
1851D	700.00	1,850.00
1851O	140.00	220.00
1852	135.00	200.00
1852C	700.00	1,750.00
1852D	750.00	2,250.00
1852O	150.00	300.00
1853	135.00	200.00

1852D 2-1/2 Dollar Gold Piece with Coronet (No Motto)

1859 2-1/2 Dollar Gold Piece with Coronet (No Motto)

	F	EF		F	EF
1853D	950.00	3,200.00	1857S	145.00	330.00
1854	135.00	200.00	1858	135.00	235.00
1854C	700.00	2,000.00	1858C	700.00	1,600.00
1854D	1,800.00	5,000.00	1859	135.00	250.00
1854O	140.00	215.00	1859D	990.00	3,000.00
1854S	32,500.00	80,000.00	1859S	180.00	900.00
1855	135.00	200.00	1860	135.00	250.00
1855C	775.00	3,000.00	1860C	700.00	1,800.00
1855D	2,000.00	7,500.00	1860S	160.00	675.00
1856	135.00	200.00	1861	135.00	200.00
1856C	700.00	2,200.00	1861S	175.00	900.00
1856D	3,510.00	9,850.00	1862, 2 over 1	450.00	1,800.00
1856O	150.00	700.00	1862	145.00	300.00
1856S	145.00	360.00	1862S	400.00	2,100.00
1857	135.00	200.00	1863 *proof only*	—	20,000.00
1857D	700.00	2,500.00	1863S	300.00	1,500.00
1857O	145.00	350.00	1864	2,500.00	11,000.00

1875 2-1/2 Dollar Gold Piece with Coronet (No Motto)

	F	EF		F	EF
1865	2,400.00	7,300.00	1879S	135.00	275.00
1865S	150.00	610.00	1880	160.00	335.00
1866	650.00	3,500.00	1881	850.00	2,750.00
1866S	170.00	650.00	1882	150.00	290.00
1867	185.00	795.00	1883	150.00	440.00
1867S	150.00	600.00	1884	150.00	400.00
1868	170.00	400.00	1885	400.00	1,700.00
1868S	135.00	350.00	1886	150.00	260.00
1869	150.00	450.00	1887	150.00	245.00
1869S	135.00	440.00	1888	140.00	225.00
1870	150.00	400.00	1889	150.00	200.00
1870S	135.00	400.00	1890	150.00	225.00
1871	150.00	325.00	1891	150.00	200.00
1871S	135.00	280.00	1892	155.00	235.00
1872	200.00	750.00	1893	145.00	190.00
1872S	135.00	400.00	1894	155.00	230.00
1873 closed 3	135.00	200.00	1895	135.00	205.00
1873 open 3	135.00	195.00	1896	135.00	195.00
1873S	135.00	400.00	1897	135.00	195.00
1874	150.00	365.00	1898	135.00	195.00
1875	1,750.00	5,000.00	1899	135.00	195.00
1875S	135.00	300.00	1900	135.00	250.00
1876	160.00	640.00	1901	135.00	195.00
1876S	145.00	500.00	1902	135.00	195.00
1877	250.00	700.00	1903	135.00	195.00
1877S	135.00	195.00	1904	135.00	195.00
1878	135.00	195.00	1905	135.00	195.00
1878S	135.00	195.00	1906	135.00	195.00
1879	135.00	195.00	1907	135.00	195.00

1911D 2-1/2 Dollar Gold Piece with Indian Head

INDIAN HEAD TYPE

	VF	AU		VF	AU
1908	160.00	190.00	1914D	160.00	190.00
1909	160.00	190.00	1915	160.00	190.00
1910	160.00	190.00	1925D	160.00	190.00
1911	160.00	190.00	1926	160.00	190.00
1911D	700.00	2,200.00	1927	160.00	190.00
1912	160.00	190.00	1928	160.00	190.00
1913	160.00	190.00	1929	160.00	190.00
1914	160.00	200.00			

3 DOLLAR GOLD PIECES

The 1851 law which lowered the rate for first class mail from five cents to three cents also authorized a three-cent coin with which to purchase the new stamps. The prevailing thought at the time continued, and in 1853 another law authorized a three-dollar gold piece, which could be used to conveniently purchase entire sheets of stamps, as well as be exchanged for 100 of the small silver trimes. Popularly called a portrait of an Indian princess, the design is more specifically that of Liberty wearing a feathered headdress, and was also used on the Type III gold dollars of 1856. It was never particularly popular, with most years outside the 1850s being struck in insignificant quantities. Mintages became almost ceremonial until striking was finally suspended in 1889.

In its day it was popularly used as jewelry, so collectors must be very careful to inspect coins for traces of solder. Look for irregularities in the reeding or discoloration near the edge. Cleaning is both a problem and a hint to other flaws such as mount marks.

Known Counterfeits: 1877 exists made by altering genuine coins of other dates. Struck counterfeits exist of virtually every date in this series.

1860S Three Dollar Gold Piece

	VF	EF		VF	EF
1854	675.00	990.00	1870	800.00	1,000.00
1854D	8,250.00	14,500.00	1870S		*unique*
1854O	1,500.00	2,700.00	1871	825.00	1,150.00
1855	700.00	1,000.00	1872	800.00	1,000.00
1855S	990.00	2,000.00	1873 closed 3	4,000.00	5,000.00
1856	700.00	1,000.00	1873 open 3 *proof only*	—	65,000.00
1856S	750.00	1,150.00	1874	700.00	950.00
1857	700.00	1,000.00	1875 *proof only*	—	175,000.00
1857S	900.00	2,700.00	1876	5,500.00	10,000.00
1858	900.00	1,450.00	1877	1,200.00	2,700.00
1859	700.00	1,000.00	1878	700.00	1,000.00
1860	750.00	1,000.00	1879	700.00	1,000.00
1860S	850.00	1,550.00	1880	750.00	1,600.00
1861	750.00	1,025.00	1881	1,200.00	2,250.00
1862	750.00	1,000.00	1882	850.00	1,000.00
1863	800.00	1,150.00	1883	800.00	1,300.00
1864	800.00	1,050.00	1884	1,150.00	1,500.00
1865	1,200.00	2,200.00	1885	1,150.00	1,500.00
1866	850.00	1,000.00	1886	1,100.00	1,700.00
1867	850.00	1,000.00	1887	700.00	1,000.00
1868	700.00	950.00	1888	750.00	1,000.00
1869	825.00	1,000.00	1889	700.00	1,000.00

5 DOLLAR GOLD PIECES

The first American gold coin to be struck was the half eagle, or $5 gold piece in 1795. Its first obverse features a bust of Liberty wearing a tall conical cap traditionally, but inaccurately, referred to by numismatists as a turban. Originally this was paired with a reverse design featuring a skinny eagle similar to that on the first dollars, but instead of standing within a wreath it is seen holding one above its head. As with the other denominations, this was replaced by a plumper heraldic eagle bearing a shield on its chest, which later was featured on all denominations other than copper. The original bust by Robert Scott was replaced in 1807 by one designed by John Reich, and was wearing a smaller cap. A reverse eagle similar, but more realistic, was paired with the new obverse. While the design and net gold content did not change for almost thirty years, the coin's diameter was at first increased and then reduced.

Through most of its history until the 1830s, the half eagle was plagued by mass meltings, being undervalued relative to its gold content, particularly by European standards. In 1834, this was remedied by reducing the coin's gold content. This was indicated to the public by the removal of the motto over the eagle on the reverse, and by a new capless Liberty head, the "Classic Head" by William Kneass. The final Coronet-type Liberty head design was a rendition by Christian Gobrecht, which continued in use from 1839 to 1908, the motto being replaced over the eagle in 1866.

In 1908, as part of the same coin design beautification program which later introduced the Walking Liberty half dollar and St. Gaudens double eagle, sculptor Bela Lyon Pratt was asked to prepare new designs for the quarter and half eagle in secret under the authority of President Theodore Roosevelt. His work showed the bust of an Indian chief on the obverse and an eagle with closed wings on the reverse. It was both controversial and innovative in that it bore its design in relief, but recessed below the surface of the coin. While some criticized it both for aesthetic reasons and for fear of it spreading germs in dirt trapped in the recesses, it proved to be a very successful method of shielding the design from wear.

Known Counterfeits: 1811, 1815 (altered), 1841O (probable), 1852C, 1854S (altered), 1858, 1870CC (altered), 1875, 1877 (altered), 1885, 1885S, 1887 Proof (altered), 1892, 1892O (altered), 1906S, 1907D, 1908 (Liberty), 1908D, 1909 Matte Proof, 1909D, 1909O, 1910D, 1914D, 1914S, and 1915D (all counterfeit), among others. Be cautious of false C mint marks altered by cutting down an authentic O mint mark. Beware of traces of solder on earlier coins from use as jewelry. Look for interruption in the pattern of edge reeding. Be cautious of cleaned coins. This is harder to detect on gold, which usually does not tone naturally.

1795 5 Dollar Gold Piece with Turban Bust and Small Eagle

TURBAN BUST/SMALL EAGLE

	F	VF		F	VF
1795	11,500.00	17,000.00	1797 16 stars	12,000.00	17,500.00
1796 6 over 5	12,000.00	17,500.00	1798	96,000.00	165,000.00
1797 15 stars	13,500.00	19,000.00			

1803/2 5 Dollar Gold Piece with Turban Bust and Heraldic Eagle

TURBAN BUST/HERALDIC EAGLE

	F	VF
1795	8,800.00	13,500.00
1797 7 over 5	8,600.00	12,500.00
1797 16 star obv.	—	... unique
1798 small 8	2,800.00	3,600.00
1798 large 8, 13 star rev.	2,700.00	3,500.00
1798 large 8, 14 star rev.	2,900.00	3,800.00
1799	2,850.00	3,500.00
1800	2,750.00	3,300.00

	F	VF
1802 2 over 1	2,750.00	3,300.00
1803 3 over 2	2,750.00	3,300.00
1804 small 8	2,750.00	3,300.00
1804 small 8 over large 8	2,750.00	3,300.00
1805	2,750.00	3,300.00
1806 pointed 6	2,800.00	3,350.00
1806 round 6	2,750.00	3,300.00
1807	2,750.00	3,300.00

1810 5 Dollar Gold Piece with Capped Bust (small date, tall 5)

CAPPED BUST TYPE

	F	VF
1807	2,000.00	2,400.00
1808 8 over 7	2,700.00	3,300.00
1808	2,000.00	2,400.00
1809 9 over 8	2,000.00	2,400.00

	F	VF
1810 small date, small 5	9,600.00	22,500.00
1810 small date, tall 5	2,100.00	2,400.00

	F	VF
1810 large date, small 5	13,500.00	25,000.00
1810 large date, large 5	2,000.00	2,400.00
1811 small 5	2,000.00	2,400.00
1811 tall 5	1,950.00	2,350.00
1812	2,000.00	2,400.00
1813	2,400.00	2,750.00
1814 4 over 3	2,500.00	2,800.00
1815	EF	70,000.00
1818	2,500.00	2,750.00
1818 STATES OF	2,700.00	2,950.00
1818 5D over 50	2,900.00	3,200.00
1819	— 9,600.00	16,500.00

	F	VF
1819 5D over 50	17,000.00	
1820 curved-base 2	2,500.00	2,800.00
1820 square-base 2	2,450.00	2,800.00
1821	7,000.00	14,000.00
1822	—	1,000,000.00
1823	2,500.00	3,400.00
1824	5,000.00	10,000.00
1825 5 over 1	5,150.00	8,250.00
1825 5 over 4	only two known	
1826	3,600.00	7,500.00
1827	5,600.00	9,600.00
1828 8 over 7	13,000.00	17,000.00
1828	5,500.00	12,500.00
1829	—extremely rare	

1834 5 Dollar Gold Piece with Classic
Head and Crosslet 4 (No Motto)

CAPPED BUST/REDUCED DIAMETER

	F	VF
1829	37,500.00	50,000.00
1830	14,500.00	17,500.00
1831	14,500.00	17,500.00
1832 12 stars	only six known	
1832 13 stars	14,500.00	17,500.00
1833	14,500.00	17,500.00
1834 plain 4	14,500.00	17,500.00
1834 crosslet 4	14,5800.00	17,500.00

CLASSIC HEAD (NO MOTTO)

	VF	EF
1834 plain 4	370.00	540.00
1834 crosslet 4	1,600.00	2,600.00
1835	370.00	550.00
1836	370.00	540.00
1837	370.00	570.00
1838	370.00	540.00
1838C	1,850.00	3,850.00
1838D	1,450.00	3,400.00

1841 5 Dollar Gold Piece with Coronet (No Motto)

1851 5 Dollar Gold Piece with Coronet (No Motto)

CORONET TYPE (NO MOTTO)

	VF	EF
1839	275.00	480.00
1839C	2,000.00	3,000.00
1839D	1,600.00	2,300.00
1840	235.00	360.00
1840C	2,000.00	2,900.00
1840D	1,500.00	3,000.00
1840O	325.00	850.00
1841	375.00	1,750.00
1841C	1,400.00	1,900.00
1841D	1,450.00	1,900.00
1841O	—	two known
1842 small letters	345.00	1,100.00
1842 large letters	750.00	2,000.00
1842C small date	9,000.00	23,000.00
1842C large date	1,400.00	2,000.00
1842D small letters	1,450.00	1,900.00
1842D large letters	2,200.00	5,800.00
1842O	1,000.00	3,000.00
1843	210.00	250.00
1843C	1,400.00	1,900.00
1843D	1,450.00	1,900.00
1843O small letters	500.00	1,800.00
1843O large letters	250.00	1,125.00
1844	220.00	240.00
1844C	1,400.00	3,000.00
1844D	1,450.00	1,900.00
1844O	250.00	375.00
1845	220.00	240.00
1845D	1,450.00	1,900.00
1845O	410.00	750.00
1846 small date	220.00	240.00
1846	220.00	240.00
1846C	1,450.00	2,900.00
1846D	1,450.00	1,900.00
1846O	200.00	375.00
1847	220.00	250.00

1858 5 Dollar Gold Piece with Coronet (No Motto)

	VF	EF		VF	EF
1847C	1,400.00	1,900.00	1856D	1,450.00	1,900.00
1847D	1,450.00	1,900.00	1856O	650.00	1,250.00
1847O	4,700.00	8,000.00	1856S	300.00	625.00
1848	225.00	275.00	1857	220.00	240.00
1848C	1,400.00	1,900.00	1857C	1,400.00	1,900.00
1848D	1,450.00	1,900.00	1857D	1,450.00	1,900.00
1849	220.00	270.00	1857O	640.00	1,400.00
1849C	1,400.00	1,900.00	1857S	300.00	525.00
1849D	1,450.00	1,900.00	1858	240.00	550.00
1850	275.00	600.00	1858C	1,400.00	1,900.00
1850C	1,400.00	1,900.00	1858D	1,450.00	1,900.00
1850D	1,450.00	1,900.00	1858S	700.00	2,350.00
1851	220.00	240.00	1859	325.00	625.00
1851C	1,400.00	1,900.00	1859C	1,400.00	1,900.00
1851D	1,450.00	1,900.00	1859D	1,450.00	1,900.00
1851O	565.00	1,500.00	1859S	1,250.00	3,500.00
1852	220.00	245.00	1860	275.00	575.00
1852C	1,400.00	1,900.00	1860C	1,400.00	2,200.00
1852D	1,450.00	1,900.00	1860D	1,450.00	2,000.00
1853	220.00	240.00	1860S	1,100.00	2,100.00
1853C	1,400.00	1,900.00	1861	220.00	245.00
1853D	1,450.00	1,900.00	1861C	1,850.00	3,900.00
1854	220.00	250.00	1861D	4,400.00	7,000.00
1854C	1,400.00	1,900.00	1861S	1,000.00	4,500.00
1854D	1,450.00	1,900.00	1862	700.00	1,850.00
1854O	300.00	525.00	1862S	3,000.00	6,300.00
1854S	—	... extremely rare	1863	1,200.00	3,750.00
1855	220.00	235.00	1863S	1,450.00	3,900.00
1855C	1,400.00	2,000.00	1864	630.00	1,850.00
1855D	1,450.00	1,900.00	1864S	6,000.00	16,000.00
1855O	650.00	2,100.00	1865	1,300.00	4,100.00
1855S	390.00	975.00	1865S	1,350.00	2,400.00
1856	220.00	240.00	1866S	1,650.00	4,000.00
1856C	1,400.00	1,900.00			

1866 5 Dollar Gold Piece with Coronet and Motto

CORONET TYPE (WITH MOTTO)

	VF	EF
1866	800.00	1,650.00
1866S	900.00	2,600.00
1867	500.00	1,600.00
1867S	1,300.00	2,700.00
1868	650.00	1,000.00
1868S	400.00	1,550.00
1869	925.00	2,300.00
1869S	500.00	1,750.00
1870	800.00	1,950.00
1870CC	5,000.00	13,000.00
1870S	950.00	2,600.00
1871	950.00	1,800.00
1871CC	1,100.00	3,3000.00
1871S	500.00	1,000.00
1872	850.00	1,900.00
1872CC	1,100.00	4,800.00
1872S	445.00	800.00
1873 closed 3	180.00	225.00
1873 open 3	180.00	215.00
1873CC	2,250.00	12,500.00
1873S	510.00	1,400.00
1874	650.00	1,650.00
1874CC	800.00	1,750.00
1874S	650.00	2,000.00
1875	34,000.00	45,000.00
1875CC	1,400.00	4,400.00
1875S	675.00	2,250.00

	VF	EF
1876	1,000.00	2,400.00
1876CC	1,200.00	5,000.00
1876S	2,000.00	3,600.00
1877	900.00	2,700.00
1877CC	1,000.00	3,300.00
1877S	390.00	650.00
1878	160.00	190.00
1878CC	3,000.00	7,300.00
1878S	165.00	190.00
1879	165.00	180.00
1879CC	525.00	1,400.00
1879S	180.00	225.00
1880	160.00	175.00
1880CC	425.00	770.00
1880S	160.00	175.00
1881 1 over 0	330.00	600.00
1881	160.00	175.00
1881CC	515.00	1,400.00
1881S	160.00	175.00
1882	160.00	175.00
1882CC	380.00	545.00
1882S	160.00	175.00
1883	160.00	175.00
1883CC	450.00	990.00
1883S	195.00	240.00
1884	170.00	200.00
1884CC	550.00	975.00

1899 5 Dollar Gold Piece with Coronet and Motto

	VF	EF		VF	EF
1884S	170.00	200.00	1896	160.00	175.00
1885	160.00	175.00	1896S	200.00	250.00
1885S	160.00	175.00	1897	160.00	175.00
1886	160.00	175.00	1897S	175.00	210.00
1886S	160.00	175.00	1898	160.00	175.00
1887 *proof only*	—	130,000.00	1898S	175.00	200.00
1887S	160.00	175.00	1899	160.00	175.00
1888	175.00	220.00	1899S	170.00	180.00
1888S	175.00	200.00	1900	160.00	175.00
1889	280.00	440.00	1900S	170.00	190.00
1890	385.00	475.00	1901	160.00	175.00
1890CC	320.00	385.00	1901S 1 over 0	165.00	200.00
1891	170.00	200.00	1901S	160.00	175.00
1891CC	310.00	410.00	1902	160.00	175.00
1892	160.00	175.00	1902S	160.00	175.00
1892CC	310.00	390.00	1903	160.00	175.00
1892O	500.00	990.00	1903S	160.00	175.00
1892S	180.00	195.00	1904	160.00	175.00
1893	160.00	175.00	1904S	175.00	215.00
1893CC	310.00	440.00	1905	160.00	175.00
1893O	215.00	310.00	1905S	170.00	190.00
1893S	170.00	200.00	1906	160.00	175.00
1894	160.00	175.00	1906D	160.00	175.00
1894O	200.00	350.00	1906S	165.00	185.00
1894S	230.00	365.00	1907	160.00	175.00
1895	160.00	175.00	1907D	160.00	175.00
1895S	200.00	275.00	1908	160.00	175.00

1908 5 Dollar Gold Piece with Indian Head

INDIAN HEAD TYPE

	VF	EF		VF	EF
1908	195.00	220.00	1911S	195.00	270.00
1908D	195.00	220.00	1912	195.00	220.00
1908S	195.00	435.00	1912S	195.00	320.00
1909	195.00	220.00	1913	195.00	220.00
1909D	195.00	220.00	1913S	200.00	290.00
1909O	650.00	2,000.00	1914	195.00	220.00
1909S	195.00	270.00	1914D	195.00	230.00
1910	195.00	220.00	1914S	260.00	300.00
1910D	195.00	220.00	1915	195.00	220.00
1910S	195.00	280.00	1915S	270.00	400.00
1911	195.00	220.00	1916S	260.00	295.00
1911D	350.00	450.00	1929	2,750.00	5,500.00

10 DOLLAR GOLD PIECES

Among the first two American gold coins to be struck was the eagle or $10 gold piece in 1795, and it was George Washington himself who received the first example. Its first obverse features a bust of Liberty by Robert Scot, wearing a tall conical cap traditionally, but inaccurately, referred to by numismatists as a turban. Originally this was paired with a reverse design featuring a skinny eagle similar to that on the first silver dollars, but instead of standing within a wreath, it is seen holding one above its head. As with the other denominations, this was replaced by a plumper heraldic eagle bearing a shield on its chest, which later was featured on all denominations other than copper.

All these early eagles were struck on a primitive screw press with hand engraved dies, no two of which were identical. Many will show evidence of adjustment marks, a scraping of metal from the blank before striking to prevent the coin from being overweight. While not desirable, they are not considered damage, as they are part of the manufacturing process.

The initial issue of 1795-1804 was plagued by mass meltings and wholesale export, being undervalued relative to its gold content, particularly by European standards. As a result, its coinage was completely suspended for more than thirty years. It was reintroduced in 1838 on the reduced gold standard adopted in 1834 to prevent these abuses. The new gold eagle featured a Liberty head wearing a coronet, Christian Gobrecht's interpretation of a painting of Venus by Benjamin West. A new, more realistic reverse eagle still wore a heraldic shield. This design continued in use until 1907, the motto being replaced over the eagle in 1866.

In 1908, as part of the same coin design beautification trend which later introduced the Walking Liberty half dollar and Mercury dime, noted sculptor Augustus St. Gaudens was asked to prepare new designs for the eagle and double eagle by President Theodore Roosevelt. His work showed the head of Liberty wearing an Indian warbonnet, the headdress being added to St. Gauden's head originally designed as Victory at the President's instruction. The reverse featured a very proud eagle with closed wings.

As Roosevelt believed the use of the motto "In God We Trust" on coinage to be a debased use of the divine name, it was omitted from the initial issues. This upset Congress so much that a law was enacted that restored it during 1908.

Known Counterfeits: 1799, 1858 (altered), 1889 (altered from Ps), 1901S, 1906D, 1906S, 1907, 1908 with Motto Proof, 1908S, 1909 Matte Proof, 1909S, 1910 Proof, 1910S, 1911 Proof, 1911D, 1911S, 1912S, 1913, 1913S, 1914S, 1915S, 1916S, 1926, 1932, 1933, among others especially 1870 to 1933. Be cautious of false C mint marks altered by cutting down an authentic O mint mark. Beware of traces of solder on earlier coins from use as jewelry. Look for interruption in the pattern of edge reeding. Be cautious of cleaned coins. This is harder to detect on gold which usually does not tone naturally.

1795 10 Dollar Gold Piece with Turban Bust and Small Eagle (13 leaves)

TURBAN BUST/SMALL EAGLE

	F	VF		F	VF
1795 9 leaves below eagle	25,000.00	40,000.00	1796	18,000.00	24,000.00
1795 13 leaves	17,000.00	22,000.00	1797	24,000.00	30,000.00

1799 10 Dollar Gold Piece

TURBAN BUST/HERALDIC EAGLE

	F	VF		F	VF
1797	8,250.00	10,000.00	1799	7,500.00	8,900.00
1798/97 9 stars l., 4 r.	9,900.00	17,500.00	1800	7,500.00	8,900.00
1798/97 7 stars l., 6 r.	20,000.00	33,000.00	1801	7,500.00	8,900.00
			1803	7,500.00	9,000.00
			1804	7,700.00	9,250.00

1849O 10 Dollar Gold Piece with Coronet (No Motto)

CORONET TYPE (NO MOTTO)

	VF	EF		VF	EF
1838	1,100.00	2,900.00	1853 3 over 2	550.00	750.00
1839 large letters	1,000.00	1,900.00	1853	300.00	350.00
1839 small letters	1,500.00	3,500.00	1853O	325.00	485.00
1840	400.00	650.00	1854	320.00	400.00
1841	385.00	500.00	1854O small date	375.00	675.00
1841O	2,200.00	5,000.00	1854O large date	475.00	875.00
1842 small date	375.00	620.00	1854S	325.00	410.00
1842 large date	325.00	475.00	1855	300.00	350.00
1842O	370.00	510.00	1855O	625.00	1,250.00
1843	370.00	490.00	1855S	1,250.00	2,200.00
1843O	370.00	470.00	1856	300.00	350.00
1844	1,350.00	2,700.00	1856O	715.00	1,200.00
1844O	325.00	475.00	1856S	320.00	500.00
1845	600.00	775.00	1857	490.00	850.00
1845O	380.00	650.00	1857O	975.00	1,850.00
1846	625.00	900.00	1857S	375.00	950.00
1846O	425.00	770.00	1858	4,650.00	7,250.00
1847	300.00	350.00	1858O	435.00	740.00
1847O	325.00	375.00	1858S	1,450.00	3,100.00
1848	340.00	375.00	1859	390.00	750.00
1848O	525.00	1,050.00	1859O	3,800.00	8,200.00
1849	300.00	350.00	1859S	1,800.00	4,500.00
1849O	710.00	2,000.00	1860	420.00	775.00
1850 large date	300.00	380.00	1860O	575.00	1,100.00
1850 small date	325.00	450.00	1860S	3,200.00	6,000.00
1850O	380.00	875.00	1861	300.00	350.00
1851	320.00	470.00	1861S	1,600.00	2,900.00
1851O	315.00	440.00	1862	525.00	1,000.00
1852	300.00	350.00	1862S	1,750.00	2,950.00
1852O	650.00	1,100.00	1863	3,650.00	9,800.00

1862S 10 Dollar Gold Piece with Coronet (No Motto)

	VF	EF		VF	EF
1863S	1,600.00	3,350.00	1865S	5,400.00	10,700.00
1864	1,600.00	4,000.00	1865S 865 over		
1864S	4,900.00	12,500.00	inverted 186	2,800.00	6,100.00
1865	1,950.00	3,500.00	1866S	2,400.00	3,300.00

1873CC 10 Dollar Gold Piece with Coronet and Motto

CORONET TYPE (WITH MOTTO)

	VF	EF		VF	EF
1866	775.00	1,650.00	1871CC	2,150.00	4,950.00
1866S	1,550.00	3,400.00	1871S	1,075.00	1,550.00
1867	1,500.00	2,600.00	1872	2,200.00	3,600.00
1867S	2,000.00	5,200.00	1872CC	3,000.00	8,900.00
1868	500.00	750.00	1872S	550.00	850.00
1868S	1,250.00	2,100.00	1873	4,500.00	9,500.00
1869	1,400.00	2,800.00	1873CC	5,000.00	12,000.00
1869S	1,500.00	2,500.00	1873S	950.00	1,950.00
1870	800.00	1,175.00	1874	275.00	290.00
1870CC	9,250.00	22,500.00	1874CC	850.00	2,500.00
1870S	1,100.00	2,500.00	1874S	1,150.00	3,250.00
1871	1,450.00	2,350.00	1875	38,000.00	53,000.00

1882O 10 Dollar Gold Piece with Coronet and Motto

	VF	EF		VF	EF
1875CC	3,700.00	8,800.00	1885S	275.00	290.00
1876	3,400.00	4,800.00	1886	275.00	290.00
1876CC	3,200.00	6,500.00	1886S	275.00	290.00
1876S	1,250.00	2,000.00	1887	275.00	290.00
1877	2,100.00	53,800.00	1887S	275.00	290.00
1877CC	2,300.00	4,750.00	1888	275.00	290.00
1877S	550.00	700.00	1888O	275.00	290.00
1878	275.00	290.00	1888S	275.00	290.00
1878CC	3,650.00	7,600.00	1889	500.00	650.00
1878S	425.00	550.00	1889S	275.00	290.00
1879	275.00	290.00	1890	275.00	290.00
1879CC	7,500.00	13,000.00	1890CC	375.00	450.00
1879O	2,300.00	3,750.00	1891	275.00	290.00
1879S	275.00	290.00	1891CC	355.00	400.00
1880	275.00	290.00	1892	275.00	290.00
1880CC	475.00	700.00	1892CC	350.00	450.00
1880O	410.00	700.00	1892O	275.00	290.00
1880S	275.00	290.00	1892S	275.00	290.00
1881	275.00	290.00	1893	275.00	290.00
1881CC	360.00	515.00	1893CC	425.00	625.00
1881O	375.00	650.00	1893O	275.00	315.00
1881S	275.00	290.00	1893S	275.00	290.00
1882	275.00	290.00	1894	275.00	290.00
1882CC	850.00	1,300.00	1894O	275.00	290.00
1882O	375.00	575.00	1894S	275.00	385.00
1882S	275.00	290.00	1895	275.00	290.00
1883	275.00	290.00	1895O	275.00	290.00
1883CC	425.00	700.00	1895S	275.00	300.00
1883O	3,000.00	6,800.00	1896	275.00	290.00
1883S	275.00	290.00	1896S	275.00	290.00
1884	275.00	290.00	1897	275.00	290.00
1884CC	600.00	950.00	1897O	275.00	290.00
1884S	275.00	290.00	1897S	275.00	290.00
1885	275.00	290.00	1898	275.00	290.00

1901 10 Dollar Gold Piece with Coronet and Motto

	VF	EF		VF	EF
1898S	275.00	290.00	1903S	275.00	290.00
1899	275.00	290.00	1904	275.00	290.00
1899O	275.00	290.00	1904O	275.00	290.00
1899S	275.00	290.00	1905	275.00	290.00
1900	275.00	290.00	1905S	275.00	290.00
1900S	275.00	290.00	1906	275.00	290.00
1901	275.00	290.00	1906D	275.00	290.00
1901O	275.00	290.00	1906O	275.00	290.00
1901S	275.00	290.00	1906S	275.00	290.00
1902	275.00	290.00	1907	275.00	290.00
1902S	275.00	290.00	1907D	275.00	290.00
1903	275.00	290.00	1907S	275.00	290.00
1903O	275.00	290.00			

1907 10 Dollar Gold Piece with Indian Head and No Motto

INDIAN HEAD/NO MOTTO

	VF	EF		VF	EF
1907 wire rim, periods	—	11,000.00	1907 no periods	350.00	375.00
1907 rounded rim, periods	—	24,000.00	1908	350.00	390.00
			1908D	335.00	375.00

1913 10 Dollar Gold Piece with Indian Head and Motto

INDIAN HEAD/WITH MOTTO

	VF	EF		VF	EF
1908	320.00	360.00	1913	320.00	335.00
1908D	320.00	360.00	1913S	550.00	640.00
1908S	360.00	390.00	1914	325.00	340.00
1909	320.00	335.00	1914D	320.00	340.00
1909D	320.00	335.00	1914S	320.00	340.00
1909S	330.00	350.00	1915	320.00	340.00
1910	335.00	375.00	1915S	550.00	700.00
1910D	330.00	365.00	1916S	330.00	350.00
1910S	330.00	370.00	1920S	5,000.00	7,250.00
1911	325.00	365.00	1926	300.00	325.00
1911D	425.00	725.00	1930S	4,000.00	6,000.00
1911S	365.00	550.00	1932	300.00	325.00
1912	330.00	335.00	1933	MS-60	80,000.00
1912S	330.00	350.00			

20 DOLLAR GOLD PIECES

The California Gold Rush of the 1840s resulted in large quantities of bullion being received at the mint for coinage. Partially to make this massive coinage more expedient and partially because of the obvious convenience of using fewer coins for large international payments, the bill proposing the introduction of gold dollars was amended to include a large $20 gold piece called a "double eagle."   James B. Longacre engraved a bust of Liberty wearing a coronet similar to, but of much more refined style, than the one in use on smaller gold since 1838. A facing heraldic eagle with a circlet of stars and a radiant arc above graced the reverse, the two motto ribbons at its sides suggesting the denomination of two eagles.

This design continued in use until 1907, the motto being placed within the circlet over the eagle in 1866. Two other minor modifications were attempted. The first (1861), called the Paquet reverse, is a subtle rearrangement of details, and for technical reasons was abandoned almost immediately. The other was the replacement in 1877 of the abbreviation D. with the word dollars.

In 1908, as part of the same coin design beautification trend which later introduced the Walking Liberty half dollar and Mercury dime, noted sculptor Augustus St. Gaudens was asked by President Theodore Roosevelt to prepare new designs for the double eagle and eagle. His work showed a full figure of Liberty, holding a torch and olive branch, striding towards the viewer. It was very much inspired by Hellenistic sculpture, as correspondence between the two men clearly confirms. The reverse featured an eagle in mid-flight with a rising sun and rays in the background.

As Roosevelt believed the use of the motto "In God We Trust" on coinage to be a debased use of the divine name, it was omitted from the initial issues. This upset Congress so much that a law was enacted replacing it during 1908. To avoid public confusion the date was changed from Roman numerals to Arabic ones, and because the initial design was of such high relief that it took three strikes by the dies, its relief was lowered as well.

Both the Liberty type and the Saint Gaudens type are often found with heavy bag marks due to their soft metal and heavy weight. Examples virtually free from bagging command a substantial premium.

Known Counterfeits: 1879, 1879O, 1881 (altered), 1882 (altered), 1887 (altered), 1891, 1894, 1897S, 1898S, 1899S, 1900, 1900S, 1901S, 1903, 1903S, 1904, 1904S, 1906, 1906S, MCMVII, 1907 (Saint-Gaudens), 1908, 1909, 1910D, 1910S, 1911D, 1914D, 1914S, 1915, 1916S, 1919, 1920, 1921, 1922, 1923, 1924, 1925, 1926, 1927, 1927D (altered), 1928, 1929, among others especially 1870 to 1932. This series generally has been extensively counterfeited, be cautious. Beware of traces of solder on earlier coins from use as jewelry. Look for interruption in the pattern of edge reeding. Be cautious of cleaned coins. This is harder to detect on gold, which usually does not tone naturally.

1850 20 Dollar Gold Piece with Liberty Head (Type I)

LIBERTY HEAD—TYPE I

	VF	EF
1849		unique
1850	700.00	1,150.00
1850O	850.00	1,400.00
1851	650.00	700.00
1851O	800.00	985.00
1852	650.00	720.00
1852O	800.00	1,000.00
1853 3 over 2	700.00	850.00
1853	650.00	720.00
1853O	750.00	1,200.00
1854	650.00	715.00
1854O	30,000.00	57,000.00
1854S	700.00	825.00
1855	650.00	725.00
1855O	2,500.00	5,900.00
1855S	675.00	750.00
1856	675.00	725.00
1856O	42,000.00	75,000.00
1856S	650.00	725.00
1857	650.00	675.00
1857O	1,050.00	1,950.00
1857S	650.00	700.00
1858	700.00	925.00
1858O	1,500.00	2,200.00

	VF	EF
1858S	650.00	800.00
1859	960.00	2,100.00
1859O	4,000.00	8,000.00
1859S	650.00	700.00
1860	650.00	700.00
1860O	3,800.00	7,500.00
1860S	750.00	900.00
1861	650.00	700.00
1861O	2,500.00	5,000.00

Most of these were struck by Louisiana and the Confederacy after withdrawal from the Union.

	VF	EF
1861S	650.00	800.00
1861 Paquet rev.	Proof-67	660,000.00
1861S Paquet rev.	11,000.00	22,000.00
1862	925.00	1,450.00
1862S	650.00	900.00
1863	720.00	880.00
1863S	650.00	850.00
1864	775.00	990.00
1864S	650.00	750.00
1865	650.00	700.00
1865S	650.00	715.00
1866S	1,950.00	3,500.00

1869S 20 Dollar Gold Piece with Liberty Head and Motto (Type II)

LIBERTY HEAD (WITH MOTTO)— TYPE II

	VF	EF		VF	EF
1866	650.00	700.00	1872CC	1,900.00	2,400.00
1866S	600.00	650.00	1872S	600.00	700.00
1867	600.00	650.00	1873 closed 3	650.00	750.00
1867S	600.00	650.00	1873 open 3	600.00	650.00
1868	800.00	1,100.00	1873CC	2,250.00	3,500.00
1868S	600.00	750.00	1873S	600.00	650.00
1869	675.00	850.00	1874	600.00	650.00
1869S	600.00	650.00	1874CC	1,100.00	1,500.00
1870	700.00	960.00	1874S	600.00	650.00
1870CC	85,000.00	115,000.00	1875	600.00	650.00
1870S	600.00	675.00	1875CC	1,100.00	1,300.00
1871	700.00	900.00	1875S	600.00	650.00
1871CC	6,000.00	9,600.00	1876	600.00	650.00
1871S	600.00	700.00	1876CC	1,100.00	1,300.00
1872	600.00	700.00	1876S	600.00	650.00

1877 20 Dollar Gold Piece with Liberty Head (Type III)

1903 20 Dollar Gold Piece with Liberty Head (Type III)

LIBERTY HEAD—TYPE III

	VF	EF		VF	EF
1877	575.00	585.00	1889CC	1,250.00	1,450.00
1877CC	1,250.00	1,550.00	1889S	575.00	585.00
1877S	575.00	585.00	1890	575.00	585.00
1878	575.00	585.00	1890CC	1,100.00	1,400.00
1878CC	2,000.00	2,800.00	1890S	575.00	585.00
1878S	575.00	585.00	1891	3,200.00	9,700.00
1879	575.00	585.00	1891CC	3,500.00	5,000.00
1879CC	2,000.00	3,000.00	1891S	575.00	585.00
1879O	4,000.00	6,750.00	1892	1,150.00	1,650.00
1879S	575.00	585.00	1892CC	1,200.00	1,400.00
1880	575.00	585.00	1892S	575.00	585.00
1880S	575.00	585.00	1893	575.00	585.00
1881	4,000.00	6,750.00	1893CC	1,400.00	1,750.00
1881S	575.00	585.00	1893S	575.00	585.00
1882	7,000.00	15,000.00	1894	575.00	585.00
1882CC	1,150.00	1,375.00	1894S	575.00	585.00
1882S	575.00	585.00	1895	575.00	585.00
1883	proof only	45,000.00	1895S	575.00	585.00
1883CC	1,100.00	1,250.00	1896	575.00	585.00
1883S	575.00	585.00	1896S	575.00	585.00
1884	proof only	71,000.00	1897	575.00	585.00
1884CC	1,100.00	1,300.00	1897S	575.00	585.00
1884S	575.00	585.00	1898	575.00	585.00
1885	6,000.00	8,000.00	1898S	575.00	585.00
1885CC	2,100.00	3,000.00	1899	575.00	585.00
1885S	575.00	585.00	1899S	575.00	585.00
1886	7,000.00	11,500.00	1900	575.00	585.00
1887	proof only	30,000.00	1900S	575.00	585.00
1887S	575.00	585.00	1901	575.00	585.00
1888	575.00	585.00	1901S	575.00	585.00
1888S	575.00	585.00	1902	575.00	585.00
1889	600.00	650.00	1902S	575.00	585.00

	VF	EF
1903	575.00	560.00
1903S	575.00	560.00
1904	575.00	560.00
1904S	575.00	560.00
1905	575.00	560.00
1905S	575.00	560.00

	VF	EF
1906	575.00	585.00
1906D	575.00	585.00
1906S	575.00	585.00
1907	575.00	585.00
1907D	575.00	585.00
1907S	575.00	585.00

1907 High Relief 20 Dollar Saint Gaudens Gold Piece with No Motto

SAINT-GAUDENS/NO MOTTO

	VF	EF
1907 high relief, wire rim	6,100.00	6,700.00
1907 high relief, flat rim	6,250.00	6,900.00

	VF	EF
1907 Arabic numerals	575.00	585.00
1908	575.00	585.00
1908D	575.00	585.00

SAINT-GAUDENS/WITH MOTTO

	VF	EF
1908	575.00	535.00
1908D	575.00	495.00
1908S	750.00	1,400.00
1909/8	575.00	580.00
1909	575.00	560.00
1909D	575.00	690.00
1909S	575.00	535.00
1910	575.00	535.00
1910D	575.00	535.00
1910S	575.00	535.00
1911	575.00	535.00
1911D	575.00	535.00
1911S	575.00	535.00

	VF	EF
1912	575.00	585.00
1913	575.00	585.00
1913D	575.00	585.00
1913S	575.00	800.00
1914	575.00	585.00
1914D	575.00	585.00
1914S	575.00	585.00
1915	575.00	585.00
1915S	575.00	585.00
1916S	575.00	585.00
1920	575.00	585.00
1920S	5,500.00	9,950.00
1921	8,000.00	15,000.00

1909 20 Dollar Saint Gaudens Gold Piece with Motto

	VF	EF		VF	EF
1922	575.00	585.00	1926S	700.00	1,300.00
1922S	575.00	750.00	1927	575.00	585.00
1923	575.00	585.00	1927D	—	195,000.00
1923D	575.00	585.00	1927S	2,500.00	5,000.00
1924	575.00	585.00	1928	575.00	585.00
1924D	800.00	1,325.00	1929	4,750.00	7,000.00
1924S	750.00	1,300.00	1930S	6,000.00	15,000.00
1925	575.00	585.00	1931	4,850.00	9,000.00
1925D	1,000.00	1,800.00	1931D	5,500.00	9,000.00
1925S	900.00	1,350.00	1932	7,000.00	10,000.00
1926	575.00	585.00	1933	*MS-65*	**7,590,000.00**
1926D	1,100.00	2,900.00			

U.S. PROOF SETS

Proof coins have their origins centuries ago when special carefully produced strikings were prepared as examples of the "ideal" coin, very often for reference or for royal approval. American proof coins are known at least from the early 1800s, but those proofs were not widely available. They were struck for VIPs and for those special collectors and coin dealers with personal connections at the mint.

As the proof coin developed through the late 19th and early 20th centuries, certain criteria began to characterize their manufacture. Generally these days, they are struck twice with highly polished dies on carefully prepared polished blanks. Early in the 20th century the dies were given a matte or sandblast finish, but this soon fell out of favor. Recently some proofs have been struck with a combination of finishes: a dull matte finish on the motifs such as portraits, with a highly reflective, mirror-like surface in the fields. These are called cameo proofs and are more desirable than conventional proofs with a mirror-like finish over the entire surface.

Beginning in 1936 the mint began the active sale of proof sets to the general public. Each set usually contains one coin of each circulating denomination. They have been released every year since with the exceptions of 1943-1949 and 1965-1967. Proof sets of the 1950s were originally sold in cardboard boxes, later in flat cellophane sheets inside a special envelope. Today they come in hard plastic cases. Proof sets not in their original holders are usually traded at a discount. Such removal can damage their fragile surfaces by exposure to breathing and humidity. Such maltreatment can cause "carbon spots" to form. This is what collectors call tiny black spots that form by this exposure.

Since the mint has begun active marketing of recent commemoratives, they have also offered special proof sets containing a commemorative dollar as well as the minor coins. These are called Prestige sets. Another option the government has offered proof set buyers since 1992 is the traditional alloy of 90% silver, despite the fact that no coins for circulation are struck in that composition. Special sets are also sold containing just the statehood quarters of that year.

Known Counterfeits: Proof sets are not generally counterfeited, but regular coins can occasionally be treated by pickling to look like matte proofs.

	PF			PF
1936	6,750.00	1960 small date cent		56.00
1937	3,600.00	1961		11.50
1938	2,000.00	1962		11.50
1939	1,850.00	1963		15.00
1940	1,550.00	1964		12.00
1941	1,550.00	1968S		8.00
1942 5 coins	1,375.00	1968S no mint mark dime		11,000.00
1942 6 coins	1,550.00	1969S		8.00
1950	700.00	1970S large date cent		16.00
1951	630.00	1970S small date cent		115.00
1952	340.00	1970S no mint mark dime		1,750.00
1953	325.00	1971S		7.00
1954	190.00	1971S no mint mark nickel		1,450.00
1955 box	150.00	1972S		5.50
1955 flat pack	200.00	1973S		13.00
1956	73.50	1974S		11.50
1957	35.00	1975S		15.50
1958	90.00	1975S no mint mark dime		50,000.00
1959	29.00	1976S		9.00
1960	20.00	1976S 3-pc. silver		18.50

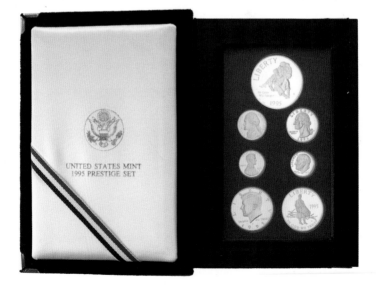

1995S Prestige Set

1999 Proof Sets

	PF			PF
1977S	8.50	1994S Silver Premier		50.00
1978S	10.00	1995S		92.00
1979S filled S	11.00	1995S Prestige		300.00
1979S clear S	130.00	1995S Silver		108.00
1980S	10.00	1995S Silver Premier		110.00
1981S	10.00	1996S		18.00
1982S	5.50	1996S Prestige		500.00
1983S	7.00	1996S Silver		52.50
1983S no mint mark dime	1,350.00	1996S Silver Premier		56.00
1983S Prestige	110.00	1997S		65.00
1984S	11.00	1997S Prestige		250.00
1984S Prestige	24.00	1997S Silver		98.00
1985S	6.00	1997S Silver Premier		100.00
1986S	20.50	1998S		38.50
1986S Prestige	32.50	1998S Silver		43.00
1987S	5.50	1998 Silver Premier		42.50
1987S Prestige	22.00	1999S		92.50
1988S	11.00	1999S Silver		285.00
1988S Prestige	32.00	1999 quarters		52.50
1989S	10.00	2000S		21.00
1989S Prestige	41.00	2000S Silver		36.00
1990S	10.00	2000S quarters		16.50
1990S no mint mark cent	8,000.00	2001S		82.50
1990S Prestige	32.00	2001S Silver		140.00
1990S Prestige, no mint mark cent	8,000.00	2001S quarters		35.50
1991S	17.50	2002S		55.00
1991S Prestige	80.00	2002S Silver		83.50
1992S	8.50	2002S quarters		25.00
1992S Prestige	160.00	2003S		35.00
1992S Silver	17.50	2003S Silver		38.00
1992S Silver Premier	17.50	2003S quarters		21.00
1993S	16.00	2004S		60.00
1993S Prestige	52.00	2004S Silver		52.00
1993S Silver	40.00	2004S quarters		32.00
1993S Silver Premier	40.00	2004S Silver quarters		35.00
1994S	25.00	2005S		36.00
1994S Prestige	60.00	2005S Silver		50.00
1994S Silver	44.00	2005S quarters		30.00
		2005S Silver quarters		35.00

U.S. MINT SETS

Mint sets do not necessarily contain coins superior to those placed in circulation. They are sold as a convenience to collectors who wish to obtain one example of each coin struck for circulation from each mint used to strike that denomination.

Mint sets from 1947 to 1958 contain two of each coin. No conventional mint sets were packaged from 1965 to 1967. The Special Mint Sets of these years were of a superior quality (despite initial government claims to the contrary) perhaps to compensate the public for the lack of proof sets available in those years. While Philadelphia, Denver and San Francisco were all striking coins for circulation, no mint marks were used so their products cannot be told apart. 1966 and 1967 sets came in rigid cases within a tight fitting cardboard box. When the use of mint marks was resumed in 1968 the coins of the different mints were separated by placing them in blue or red plastic sleeves. Some recent mint sets also contain commemoratives. In 1982 and 1983 souvenir sets sold at the mint replaced mint sets.

Even more than with proof sets, mint sets must be in their original packaging to command a premium above loose, uncirculated coins. Removing them from their protective packaging can damage mint state coins by exposure to breathing and humidity. Such maltreatment can cause "carbon spots" to form, much as they do on proof coins.

Known Counterfeits: When mint sets are presented in unofficial holders be careful that a slightly circulated coin is not inserted in hopes of passing it off among the others. Coins that originally constituted a mint set and have been simply placed in another holder will usually have matching toning typical of early sets. The plastic holders of 1966 and 1967 can easily be opened and other coins substituted.

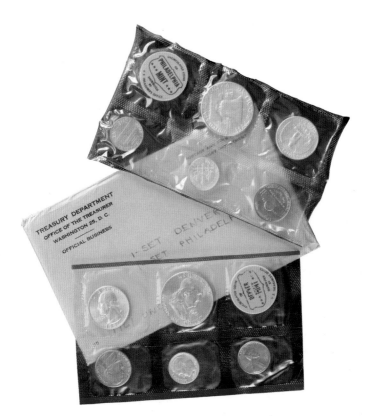

1961 Mint Set

	PF		PF
1947	1,300.00	1959	50.00
1948	600.00	1960	27.50
1949	900.00	1961	45.00
1950	none released	1962	19.50
1951	800.00	1963	15.00
1952	750.00	1964	11.50
1953	550.00	1965 Special Mint Set	12.50
1954	290.00	1966 Special Mint Set	14.00
1955	170.00	1967 Special Mint Set	21.00
1956	165.00	1968	5.00
1957	250.00	1969	7.00
1958	160.00	1970	22.00

2000D Mint Set

2001 1 oz. Silver Walking Liberty Dollar

	PF		PF
1970 small date cent	52.50	1987	8.00
1971	4.00	1988	8.00
1972	4.00	1989	7.00
1973	24.00	1990	7.00
1974	8.00	1991	12.00
1975	11.00	1992	7.00
1976	10.00	1993	11.50
1976S 3-pc. silver	17.00	1994	11.50
1977	8.50	1995	27.00
1978	10.00	1996	22.00
1979	7.00	1997	23.00
Above set was incomplete in that it lacks the Susan B. Anthony dollar.		1998	17.00
		1999	35.00
1980	7.00	2000	15.50
1981	15.00	2001	25.00
1982	*Souvenir Sets only*	2002	17.00
1983	*Souvenir Sets only*	2003	30.00
1984	6.00	2004	80.00
1985	8.00	2005	35.00
1986	22.00		

UNITED STATES PAPER MONEY

INTRODUCTION

Before the Civil War, there was no such thing as United States government paper money. During the Revolutionary War the states and the Continental Congress printed so much paper money to finance their expenses that its value evaporated, and it became nearly worthless. As a result, when the Constitution was written it contained the words "No state shall...make anything but gold and silver coin a tender in payment of debts. (1§10)." Because of this, the government avoided issuing paper money until the Civil War, and even then it was issued under limited circumstances. The first type of paper money, Demand Notes, even bore interest.

Most of the paper money issued by the United States over the following century was redeemable for gold or silver. There are many different kinds of American paper money, as the following sections will show. Their names, usually found at the top of the note as a heading, and often the colors of their seals indicate the law that authorized their issue and the nature of their backing.

Almost all United States paper currency bears a date, but this is not necessarily the year it was actually printed. It was the year of the act authorizing the series or the year the series went into production. The signature combinations on banknotes can often be used to date them.

Originally paper money was larger than today. Until 1928 they were about 7-1/2" by 3-1/8". Beginning with the series of 1928 (released 1929) they have been 6-1/8" x 2-5/8". The fractional notes of the Civil War were smaller than current notes, but varied in size.

GRADING PAPER MONEY

State of preservation is as important for paper money as it is for coins. Paper money is primarily graded to describe the amount of wear. Other factors can influence value though. Many of the terms used to describe the grades of paper money are the same as for coins. Of course the physical nature of paper requires a whole different set of definitions. They are briefly described here.

Crisp Uncirculated (CU)—This note is as pristine as when issued. It is literally crisp, with sharply pointed corners. It must have absolutely no folds, tears, or edge rounding. It can have no stains or staple holes either.

Extremely Fine (XF)—This is a particularly nice note with only the slightest sign of wear. It will still be crisp to the touch. Slight rounding of the corner points is possible, but no significant folds or creases. No tears, stains or staple holes at all.

A convenient method of detecting creases in a note is to hold the note pointed at a narrow light source and look at it from an acute angle, though not directly in the direction of the light.

Very Fine (VF)—This is a nice clean note with obvious, but moderate, signs of wear. Creases which break the ink will be visible, but generally only one in each direction, and neither crease too deep. Its corner points will be dull. While not limp, it will have only some of the crispness of better grade notes. No significant stains are visible.

Fine (F)—This is a worn, but not worn-out note. It has no crispness left. It will have heavy creases, but none that threaten the structural integrity of the note. Its edges may not be perfectly smooth, but are not irregularly worn. Trivial ink marks and smudges are acceptable.

Very Good (VG)—This note is worn and limp. It has serious deep creases. The edges are worn and not even. Some ink marks or smudges are visible. Tiny tears may be present, but no parts missing. Small staple or pin holes are acceptable.

Good (G)—This condition is not considered collectible for most purposes. Only the rarest of notes in this grade could find a home with most collectors. It is usually limp, heavily creased, stained, ripped, and pinned or stapled. Some of the creases will permit spots of light to shine through the note at their intersections.

HANDLING AND TREATMENT OF PAPER MONEY

The most important thing to know about handling currency is to **never fold paper money**. This instantaneously reduces its value. When in doubt as to whether a note has value or not, place it flat in a book until you can consult a numismatist or coin dealer. Do not carry an interesting note around in your wallet. When handling a note remember that its most fragile parts are its corners. Never touch them. Also never repair a tear in a note with tape. The tape usually is a greater detriment to the note's value than the tear. Attempts to clean a note are also likely to cause damage.

DETECTING COUNTERFEIT PAPER MONEY

Detecting counterfeit notes is not as difficult or as mysterious a business as many presume. Also many of the methods used by merchants are so inefficiently used as to be of no value.

First it must be realized that almost since its beginning, United States Paper money has been printed not on paper, but on cloth. It is part cotton and part linen with some silk. The silk is in the form of minute red and blue threads which dive in and out of the surface of the note. A color copier may be able to reproduce the colors of these tiny threads, but it cannot reproduce the texture of them entering and leaving the surface of the note. Use a magnifying glass. Another key to detecting counterfeits is crispness of the ink in the design. Images and lines should be sharp and distinct.

Minimal effort looking for these clues can catch most circulating counterfeits. Most counterfeit bills passed in circulation are accepted not because the counterfeits are deceptive, but because little or no effort is put into looking to see if they are real at all. This is entertainingly illustrated by the occasional news story about the cashier who accepts a spoof note in payment.

In recent years, Federal Reserve Notes have incorporated many new counterfeit detection devices. These are fully described in that section.

Real notes have been used occasionally to create counterfeits. A counterfeiter will take the value numbers from the corners of a note and glue them to a note of a lower face value. Such notes will often feel too thick or irregular at the corners. More importantly, such a criminal is presuming the recipients will pay virtually no attention to the notes they are accepting. Such counterfeits can be detected by even the quickest comparison with a real note.

Certain practices are designed to take an authentic note and make it appear to be in a better grade of preservation than it is. These include ironing a note to make it look less worn, and expertly gluing tears. Hold your note up to a light. Light will pass through the glue differently than through normal currency.

When choosing a rare currency dealer it is good to make sure that they have the skills to know a note is real, and the ethics to accept it back if it is not. Of course the same principles apply as mentioned above

in choosing a coin dealer. In addition to the organizations mentioned above, there are specialized organizations which also enforce codes of ethics. Two of the largest are the International Banknote Society (IBNS) and the Professional Currency Dealers Association (PCDA). These insignia in advertising indicate that the dealer is a member.

DEMAND NOTES

The demand notes of 1861 were the very first regular paper money issued by the United States. They were put into circulation under the emergency circumstances of the Civil War. The bad experiences of the overproduction of paper money during the Revolutionary War were still remembered, so limits were set on the uses of these notes. They differed from modern currency mostly in that they were not properly legal tender, but rather were "receivable in payment for all public dues." That is to say they were not good for "all debts public and private," and not by initial obligation for any private debts at all. One could use them to pay taxes, but did not have to accept them otherwise. Later a law was passed requiring their acceptance. Their name Demand Note derives from another phrase on their face, "The United States promises to pay to the bearer on demand."

On the other hand, there were limits as to how they could be redeemed. These notes were issued at five cities and could only be redeemed by the Assistant Treasurers in the individual note's specific city of issue. Designs were uniform from city to city. The $5 note shows at left the statue of Columbia from the Capitol building, a portrait of Alexander Hamilton right. The $10 shows Lincoln, then in office, left, an eagle centered, and an allegorical figure of Art right. The $20 depicts Liberty holding a sword and shield.

The nickname "green back" for paper money began with these notes, which have a distinctive green back. The privately issued paper money circulating until then had blank backs.

There are two major varieties of these, resulting from the government being ill prepared for the practical reality of hand signing millions of notes. The original intent was that clerks would be able to sign them "N. for the" Register of the Treasury and "N. for the" Treasurer of the

United States. The time it took to sign the words "for the" millions of times quickly became excessive, so the notes were modified so the words were printed on instead. The earlier varieties are worth more than the prices listed here.

High-grade notes in this series are very rare.

Known Counterfeits: Examine detail, check to make sure notes are hand signed, and use reasonable caution.

Philadelphia 5 Dollar Demand Note, Series 1861

	G	VG		G	VG
$5 Boston	450.00	3,500.00	$10 Boston	700.00	2,200.00
$5 Cincinnati	—	rare	$10 Cincinnati	—	rare
$5 New York	450.00	3,500.00	$10 New York	700.00	2,200.00
$5 Philadelphia	450.00	3,500.00	$10 Philadelphia	700.00	2,200.00
$5 St. Louis	1,000.00	1,500.00	$10 St. Louis	2,500.00	6,500.00

2 Dollar Treasury Note, Series 1890

	G	VG		G	VG
$20 Boston	5,500.00	13,500.00	$20 New York	5,500.00	13,500.00
$20 Cincinnati	—	rare	$20 Philadelphia	5,500.00	13,500.00

TREASURY NOTES

These notes, designated "Treasury Notes" by the titles on their face inscriptions, are also called "Coin Notes." This was because according to law the Secretary of the Treasury was instructed to redeem these notes in coin, either gold or silver, at his choosing. Interestingly they were not actually backed by coin at all, but rather by silver bullion.

This series was of very short duration, being issued only in 1890 and 1891. Both years have the same face designs, generally of military heroes. The original reverse designs featured the values spelled out in large letters. For 1891, they were redesigned to allow more blank space. The ornamentation of the two 0s in 100 on the reverse of the $100 notes is reminiscent of the pattern on the skin of a watermelon, hence they are known by the collecting community as "watermelon notes."

Known Counterfeits: Examine detail, silk threads in paper and use reasonable caution.

10 Dollar Treasury Note, Series 1890

	F	XF		F	XF
$1 1890			$5 1891 same	350.00	750.00
Edwin M. Stanton.	500.00	1,300.00	$10 1890 Gen. Philip H.		
$1 1891 same	250.00	450.00	Sheridan	900.00	2,500.00
$2 1890 Gen. James D.			$10 1891 same	550.00	1,300.00
McPherson	780.00	3,200.00	$20 1890 John		
$2 1891 same	400.00	950.00	Marshall	3,350.00	7,350.00
$5 1890 Gen. George H.			$20 1891 same	3,300.00	7,500.00
Thomas	500.00	2,400.00			

10 Dollar Treasury Note, Series 1890

	F	XF		F	XF
$50 1891 William H. Seward			$100 1891 same..	50,000.00	100,000.00
	22,000.00	50,000.00	$1000 1890 Gen. George Meade		
$100 1890 Adm. David G. Farragut				—	rare
	50,000.00	100,000.00	$1000 1891 same	—	rare

NATIONAL BANK NOTES

National bank notes are a hybrid of government issued and private paper money. The notes, titled "National Currency" on their face, were issued by individual private banks, but printed by the U.S. government. Not every bank could issue them, only "national banks." To qualify each bank had to meet certain criteria, which included keeping a predetermined value of U.S. government bonds on deposit with the United States Treasurer. In exchange for this commitment, the notes issued by any bank were considered legal tender of the United States and were good anywhere United States currency was good. The Treasury would stand behind these notes.

Designs did not vary from bank to bank, but they used those types designated by the Treasury. The face of each note would indicate the issuing bank's name (usually including the word "national") and its charter number. Many earlier notes would also show the coat of arms of its native state.

Each of over 1,300 issuing banks was assigned a charter number. There were three periods under which banks could apply for a twenty-year charter. The first period was 1863-1882. Those banks securing their charters during this period could issue notes of the first charter reverse design as late as 1902. Those banks receiving their charters from 1882 to 1902, the second period, issued notes of a new type back designed for second charter banks. These were actually printed 1882 to 1922. Those banks receiving their charters during the third period of authorization, 1902 to 1922, issued yet a third series of different designs from 1902 to 1929. It is seen that this system determines the design (and often apparent "date") on a note not by when it was issued, but by when the issuing bank first received its charter. Hence, different designs of a National Bank Note could be issued at the same time with different dates! A very confusing situation.

Just like all other currency, Nationals were reduced in size in 1929. Type 1 notes (1929-33) have the charter number on the face twice. Type 2 notes (1933-35) have it four times. When, in May 1935, the Treasury recalled many of the bonds which the national banks were using as security, National Bank Notes ceased to be issued.

Nationals have been among the most sought-after notes in a generally active U.S. paper money market. Not all nationals of a given type are worth the same, as certain states and cities are more popularly collected than others. Also, some banks ordered very small quantities of notes. The values below are for the most common and least expensive banks issuing that type of note. Large-size nationals from Alaska, Arizona, Hawaii, Idaho, Indian Territory, Mississippi, Nevada, New Mexico, Puerto Rico, and South Dakota are automatically worth more. The same is true for small-size nationals from Alaska, Arizona, Hawaii, Idaho, Montana, Nevada, and Wyoming.

Known Counterfeits: Examine detail, silk threads in paper and use reasonable caution.

2 Dollar National Bank Note, First Charter, Series 1875

FIRST CHARTER (1863-1875)

	VG	VF
$1 Allegory of Concord/Pilgrims landing, ND		
(Original series)	700.00	1,100.00
same, 1875	700.00	1,100.00

	VG	VF
$2 Lazy 2/Sir Walter Raleigh, ND		
(Original series)	2,900.00	4,300.00
same, 1875	2,900.00	4,300.00

	VG	VF
$5 Columbus sighting land/landing of Columbus, ND (Original series).		
	990.00	1,700.00
same, 1875	990.00	1,700.00

	VG	VF
$10 Franklin experimenting with lightning/DeSoto, ND		
(original series)	1,200.00	2,100.00
same, 1875	1,200.00	2,100.00

10 Dollar National Bank Note, First Charter, Series 1875

	VG	VF
$20 Battle of Lexington/baptism of Pocahontas, ND (original series)	1,800.00	2,750.00
same, 1875	1,800.00	2,750.00
$50 Washington Crossing Delaware and at prayer/Pilgrims, ND (original series)	8,500.00	15,000.00

	VG	VF
$100 Battle of Lake Erie/signing of the Declaration of Independence, ND (original series)	9,900.00	18,500.00
$500	—	unique
$1,000	—	unique

5 Dollar National Bank Note, Brown Back
with Charter Numbers, Second Charter, Series 1872

5 Dollar National Bank Note,
with Large *1882* 1908*, Second Charter, Series 1882

5 Dollar National Bank Note, Value Back
with Large Spelled-Out Value, Second Charter, Series 1882

SECOND CHARTER/SERIES OF 1882
"Brown Backs" with charter number

	VG	VF
$5 James Garfield	550.00	750.00
$10 as 1st charter	700.00	1,100.00
$20 as 1st charter	885.00	1,300.00
$50 as 1st charter	3,400.00	4,700.00
$100 as 1st charter	5,500.00	7,000.00

SECOND CHARTER/ SERIES OF 1882
"Value Backs" large spelled-out value

	VG	VF
$5 James Garfield	550.00	750.00
$10 as 1st charter	700.00	1,100.00
$20 as 1st charter	885.00	1,300.00
$50 as 1st charter	36,000.00	50,000.00
$100 as 2nd series	85,000.00	*extremely rare*

SECOND CHARTER/SERIES OF 1882
*"Date Backs" with large "1882*1908"*

	VG	VF
$5 James Garfield	550.00	750.00
$10 as 1st charter	700.00	1,100.00
$20 as 1st charter	885.00	1,300.00
$50 as 1st charter	3,400.00	4,700.00
$100 as 1st charter	5,500.00	7,000.00

50 Dollar National Bank Note, Third Charter, Series 1902

50 Dollar National Bank Note, Third Charter, Series 1902

5 Dollar Small Size, Type 2 National Bank Note
(serial number and bank number in brown), Series 1929

THIRD CHARTER/SERIES OF 1902
Red Treasury Seal on face

	VG	VF
$5 Benjamin Harrison/Pilgrims landing	550.00	750.00
$10 William McKinley/Columbia between ships	700.00	1,100.00
$20 Hugh McCulloch/Columbia and Capitol	885.00	1,300.00
$50 John Sherman/ train	3,400.00	4,700.00
$100 John Knox/eagle on shield	5,500.00	7,000.00

THIRD CHARTER/SERIES OF 1902
Blue Treasury Seal, "1902-1908" on back

	VG	VF
$5 as red seals	200.00	300.00
$10 as red seals	200.00	300.00
$20 as red seals	200.00	300.00
$50 as red seals	1,300.00	1,800.00
$100 as red seals	1,800.00	2,500.00

THIRD CHARTER/SERIES OF 1902
Blue Treasury Seal, "Plain Backs" without dates

	VG	VF
$5 as red seals	200.00	300.00
$10 as red seals	200.00	300.00
$20 as red seals	200.00	300.00
$50 as red seals	1,300.00	1,800.00
$100 as red seals	1,800.00	2,500.00

50 Dollar Small Size National Bank Note, Type 2, Series 1929

THIRD CHARTER/SERIES OF 1929
Brown Treasury Seal, Small-Size Notes

	VG	VF		VG	VF
$5 Type 1	100.00	120.00	$20 Type 2	110.00	120.00
$5 Type 2	100.00	120.00	$50 Type 1	340.00	380.00
$10 Type 1	100.00	120.00	$50 Type 2	340.00	380.00
$10 Type 2	100.00	120.00	$100 Type 1	480.00	550.00
$20 Type 1	110.00	120.00	$100 Type 2	480.00	600.00

NATIONAL GOLD BANK NOTES

These notes were like National Bank Notes, but they were specifically redeemable in gold coin. They were a co-operative issue of the individual National Gold Bank which held the obligation, and the U.S. Treasury. Every bank had to be a regular national bank as well, and meet all the reserve requirements. But these national banks were authorized by the Treasury to issue notes redeemable in gold.

The reason for their issue from 1870-75 was to relieve the banks in California of the daily handling of massive quantities of gold coin. All but one of the banks authorized to issue these was located in California. The very design of these notes reflects their backing by gold. Their paper is a golden yellow, and the reverse bears an array of United States gold coins of every denomination. Their remarkably fine engraving gives the coins a very realistic appearance. Because other types of notes were not very popular in California, these notes got some very hard use, and today are rare in all but worn-out condition.

Known Counterfeits: Examine detail, and look for correct yellow paper, which occasionally may tone down. Use reasonable caution.

	G	F
$5 Columbus sighting land	950.00	2,400.00
$10 Franklin experimenting with lightning	2,500.00	4,800.00
$20 Battle of Lexington	4,000.00	10,000.00

	G	F
$50 Washington crossing Delaware and at prayer	15,000.00	rare
$100 Battle of Lake Erie	38,000.00	rare

UNITED STATES NOTES

While most of these notes will carry the title "United States Note" at the top or bottom of their face, some earlier ones actually say "Treasury Note" instead. The very first notes omit both. They are, however, the same according to the legislation that authorized them. They are the longest lasting kind of American paper money, being issued for over a century, from 1862 until 1966. There are a great many different designs, of which the "Bison Ten" is the most famous and most popular. Just like all other currency, United States Notes were reduced in size with the "series of 1928" in 1929. Small-size notes are occasionally found in circulation today, and are characterized by a red Treasury seal. The latter, when worn, are not generally considered collectible.

This series includes popular "star" notes. These are notes with part of the serial number replaced by a star. They were printed to replace notes accidentally destroyed in manufacturing. These were introduced first on $20 notes in 1880 and eventually descended to $1 notes by 1917. They usually are worth more.

Known Counterfeits: Examine detail, silk threads in paper and use reasonable caution. In addition to counterfeits made to fool collectors, early circulation counterfeits of the 1863 $50, 1869 $50, and 1863 $100 exist.

2 Dollar Large Size United States Note, Series 1875

	F	XF
$1 1862 Salmon P. Chase, red seal	400.00	800.00
$1 1869 Washington, Columbus scene/ US intertwined	400.00	900.00
$1 1874-1917 same/ large X	85.00	95.00
$1 1923 Washington bust	95.00	150.00
$2 1862 Alexander Hamilton double circle	600.00	1,600.00
$2 1869 Jefferson and Capitol/II•2•TWO	600.00	1,600.00
$2 1874-1917 same/II•TWO omitted	90.00	150.00
$5 1862 Statue of Columbia l., Alexander Hamilton r.	445.00	830.00
$5 1863 same, different obligation on back	445.00	830.00

5 Dollar Large Size United States Note, Series 1869

	F	XF
$5 1869 Jackson l., pioneer family center/ circle with 5	400.00	840.00
$5 1875-1907 same, red seal/ circle with concentric pattern	110.00	230.00

10 Dollar Large Size United States Note, Series 1862

	F	XF
$5 1880 same, brown seal	195.00	540.00
$10 1862 Lincoln and allegory of Art	850.00	2,200.00
$10 1862-63 same, different obligation on back	850.00	2,200.00

10 Dollar Large Size United States Note, Series 1901

	F	XF
$10 1869 Daniel Webster and Pocahontas/inscription centered	600.00	1,300.00
$10 1875-80 same/inscription at right	390.00	780.00
$10 1880 same, brown seal	435.00	940.00
$10 1901 Bison/Columbia standing between pillars	560.00	1,200.00
$10 1923 Andrew Jackson/value	800.00	1,800.00
$20 1862 Liberty with sword and shield	1,900.00	4,200.00
$20 1862-63 same, different obligation on back	1,900.00	4,200.00
$20 1869 Alexander Hamilton l.,Victory standing r.	1,950.00	3,600.00
$20 1875-80 same/no inscription at center	400.00	900.00
$20 1880 same, brown seal	1,200.00	3,000.00

	F	XF
$50 1862 Alexander Hamilton	9,000.00	22,500.00
$50 1862-63 same, different obligation on back	8,250.00	22,000.00
$50 1869 Peace and Henry Clay	14,500.00	40,000.00
$50 1874-80 Franklin and Columbia	2,800.00	6,000.00
$50 same, brown seal	4,100.00	7,100.00
$100 1862 Eagle	15,000.00	34,000.00
$100 1862-63 same, different obligation on back	15,000.00	34,000.00
$100 1869 Lincoln and allegory of Architecture/inscription centered	14,500.00	30,000.00
$100 1875-80 same, inscription at left	4,500.00	15,000.00
$100 1880, same, brown seal	6,000.00	20,000.00
$500 1862 Albert Gallatin—		rare

1 Dollar Small Size United States Note, Red Seal, Series 1928

	F	XF
$500 1862-63 same, different obligation on back............ —		rare
$500 1869 John Quincy Adams .... —		rare
$500 1874-80 Gen. Joseph Mansfield .... —		rare
$500 1880 same, brown seal .... —		rare
$1000 1862 Robert Morris .... —		rare
$1000 1862-63 same, different obligation on back............ —		rare
$1000 1869 Columbus and DeWitt Clinton/inscription centered............ —		rare
$1000 1878-80 same, inscription at left................ —		rare
$1000 1880 same, brown seal .... —		rare

SMALL SIZE NOTES—RED SEAL

$1 1928 Washington/ONE
$2 1928-63A Jefferson/Monticello
$5 1928-63 Lincoln/Lincoln Memorial
$100 1966-66A Franklin/Indep. Hall

	F	XF
$1 1928	55.00	130.00
$2 1928	13.50	25.00
$2 1928A	45.00	95.00
$2 1928B	60.00	255.00
$2 1928C	13.00	27.00
$2 1928D	10.00	16.00
$2 1928E	15.00	30.00
$2 1928F	5.00	18.00
$2 1928G	5.00	15.00

5 Dollar Small Size United States Note, Red Seal, Series 1928

	CU
$2 1953	10.00
$2 1953A	10.00
$2 1953B	10.00
$2 1953C	10.00
$2 1963	8.00
$2 1963A	10.00

	F	XF
$5 1928	12.00	30.00
$5 1928A	15.00	40.00
$5 1928B	12.00	25.00
$5 1928C	12.00	25.00
$5 1928D	30.00	75.00
$5 1928E	10.00	20.00
$5 1928F	10.00	20.00
$5 1953	8.50	15.00
$5 1953A	7.00	12.00
$5 1953B	7.00	12.00
$5 1953C	7.50	15.00
$5 1963	7.00	12.00

	XF	CU
$100 1966	200.00	400.00
$100 1966A	350.00	1,000.00

GOLD CERTIFICATES

As the title on these notes implies, these were notes both backed by reserves in gold coin and payable to the bearer in that coin. The first Gold Certificates were issued in 1865-75, but were used for transactions between banks. Notes of this period not listed below are not known to have survived. The issue of 1882 was the first for general circulation. Again the issues of 1888-89 were only of $5,000 and $10,000 and not widely circulated. Regular issues were again placed in circulation in 1905-07. This series includes a $20 note so beautifully colored with black, red and gold ink on white gold-tinted paper that it has come to have the nickname of "Technicolor." Those of the series of 1913-28 are the most common Gold Certificates.

Like all other notes of the 1928 series, these gold certificates were printed on the reduced size paper still used today. These are distinguished from other kinds of small-size notes by a gold Treasury seal. The final issues, those of 1934, were again just for bank transactions. The government recalled these notes from general circulation in 1933 when it withdrew gold coinage. Today, they are perfectly legal to own but far scarcer due to this earlier destruction.

Known Counterfeits: Examine detail, on 1882 and later silk threads in paper, and use reasonable caution.

20 Dollar Gold Certificate, Series 1882

FIRST ISSUE—1863

$20 Eagle on shield . . . — *extremely rare*
$100 Eagle on shield . . — *extremely rare*

SECOND ISSUE—1870-71

No notes known to have survived.

THIRD ISSUE—1870S

$100 Thomas H. Benton— *extremely rare*

FOURTH ISSUE—SERIES OF 1882

	F	XF
$20 James Garfield	3,500.00	10,000.00
$50 Silas Wright	1,250.00	3,500.00
$100 Thomas Benton	900.00	2,500.00
$500 Abraham Lincoln	7,000.00	25,000.00
$1000 Alexander Hamilton	—	*rare*
$5000 James Madison	—	*rare*
$10,000 Andrew Jackson	—	*rare*

FIFTH ISSUE—SERIES OF 1888

	F	XF
$5000 James Madison	—	*rare*
$10,000 Andrew Jackson	—	*rare*

20 Dollar Gold Certificate, Series 1922

SIXTH ISSUE—SERIES OF 1900

	F	XF
$10,000 Jackson		
. . . . cut cancelled **1,400.00**		

SEVENTH ISSUE— SERIES OF 1905-07

	F	XF
$10 Michael Hillegas . **150.00** . . . **340.00**		
$20 Washington 1905 "technicolor note"		
. . . . **1,250.00** . **3,800.00**		
$20 Washington 1906		
. . . .**230.00** . . . **535.00**		

EIGHTH ISSUE—SERIES OF 1907

	F	XF
$1000 Alexander Hamilton		
. . . . **10,000.00** . . . .*rare*		

NINTH ISSUE—SERIES OF 1913

	F	XF
$50 Ulysses S. Grant .**720.00** . **1,350.00**		

TENTH ISSUE—SERIES OF 1922

	F	XF
$10 Michael Hillegas . **150.00** . . . **330.00**		
$20 Washington . . . . .**250.00** . . . **450.00**		
$50 Ulysses S. Grant .**650.00** . **1,250.00**		
$100 Thomas Benton .**650.00** . **1,700.00**		
$500 Abraham Lincoln. . . . —. . . . .*rare*		
$1000 Alexander Hamilton		
. . . .—. . . . .*rare*		

10 Dollar Small Size Gold Certificate, Series 1928

SMALL SIZE—SERIES OF 1928

	F	XF
$10 Alex. Hamilton	70.00	125.00
$20 Andrew Jackson	95.00	150.00
$50 Ulysses S. Grant	400.00	650.00
$100 Ben. Franklin	500.00	850.00

	F	XF
$500 W. McKinley	2,500.00	8,000.00
$1000 G. Cleveland	2,800.00	9,000.00
$5000 James Madison	—	rare

SILVER CERTIFICATES

On the same day, February 28, 1878, as the authorization by Congress for the striking of millions of silver dollars, it also passed legislation authorizing Silver Certificates. This is not pure coincidence. Silver Certificates were not simply backed up by silver bullion, but represented actual silver dollars held by the Treasury. The issue of this series of notes was what in part made it necessary to strike millions of Morgan dollars, and was ultimately prompted by heavy lobbying by the silver mining industry.

Some of the most famous or beautiful banknotes issued by the U.S. are Silver Certificates. These include the "Educational" $1, $2, and $5 of 1896, the "Onepapa Five," and the "Porthole Five." The name "Onepapa Five" is a misnomer. It depicts Chief Running Antelope of the Uncpapa Sioux, but because the name sounded so unfamiliar to early collectors it was quickly mispronounced "Chief One Papa."

Just like all other currency, Silver Certificates were reduced in size with the "series of 1928" in 1929.

During World War II there was fear that supplies of U.S. currency would fall into enemy hands if certain territories were overrun. The response to this was to make sure that notes distributed in these territories had distinguishing features that permitted their identification and repudiation if captured. Those Silver Certificates issued to troops in North Africa were printed with a yellow Treasury seal instead of a blue one. Notes distributed in Hawaii feature the word HAWAII overprinted very large on the back.

The motto "In God We Trust" was added to the one-dollar note for the 1935 G and H and all 1957 series. They continued to be issued until the 1957B series in 1963. Small-size silver certificates are occasionally found in circulation today and are easily recognized by a blue Treasury seal. These notes when worn are not generally considered collectible, but do have some novelty value. They have not been able to be redeemable for silver dollars since 1968.

This series includes popular "star" notes. These are notes with part of the serial number replaced by a star. They are printed to replace notes accidentally destroyed in the manufacturing process. These were introduced first in 1899. They often, but not always, are worth somewhat more.

Known Counterfeits: Examine detail, silk threads of in paper and use reasonable caution. Circulating counterfeits exist for this series and are slightly less dangerous.

1 Dollar Large Size Silver Certificate, Series 1896

	F	XF
$1 1886 Martha Washington/inscription in oval	275.00	700.00
$1 1891 same/inscription in rosette	300.00	650.00
$1 1896 History instructing youth/George and Martha Washington	340.00	630.00
$1 1899 Eagle	85.00	160.00
$1 1923 Washington	40.00	50.00
$2 1886 Gen. Winfield Scott Hancock	580.00	1,270.00

2 Dollar Large Size Silver Certificate, Series 1896

	F	XF
$2 1891 Sen. William Windom	465.00	1,350.00
$2 1896 Science Presenting Steam and Electricity to Commerce and Industry/Fulton and Morse	560.00	1,800.00

	F	XF
$2 1899 Washington, Mechanics and Agriculture	250.00	435.00

5 Dollar Large Size Silver Certificate, Series 1899

	F	XF
$5 1886 Ulysses S. Grant/Morgan silver dollars	730.00	2,500.00
$5 1891 same/inscription	510.00	1,375.00
$5 1896 Winged Electricity lighting the World	1,000.00	2,850.00

	F	XF
$5 1899 Chief "Onepapa"	480.00	995.00
$5 1923 Lincoln in porthole-like frame/great seal	500.00	1,200.00

10 Dollar Large Size Silver Certificate, 1891 Series

	F	XF
$10 1878-80 Robert Morris/S I L V E R ....**1,450.00** . **3,600.00**		
$10 1886 Thomas Hendricks in tombstone-like frame ....**700.00** . **2,600.00**		
$10 1891-1908 same/UNITED STATES in oval ....**410.00** . **1,250.00**		
$20 1878-80 Capt. StephenDecatur/ S I L V E R.......**3,500.00 10,000.00**		
$20 1886 Daniel Manning/double diamond........**3,300.00** . **7,500.00**		
$20 1891 same/double circle ....**990.00** . **2,300.00**		
$50 1878-80 Edward Everett/ S I L V E R.......**8,000.00 30,000.00**		
$50 1891 same/inscription in center ....**2,300.00** . **4,500.00**		
$100 1878-80 James Monroe/ S I L V E R......**10,000.00 33,000.00**		
$100 1891 same/inscription in center **7,500.00 15,000.00**		
$500 1878-80 Sen. Charles Sumner/ S I L V E R..........— ....*rare*		
$1000 1878-80 William Marcy ....— ....*rare*		
$1000 1891 Columbia and Marcy ....— ....*rare*		

1 Dollar Small Size Silver Certificate, Blue Seal, Series 1928

SMALL SIZE NOTES—BLUE SEAL

$1 1928-28E Washington/ONE
$1 1934-57B Washington/Great Seal
$5 1934-53C Lincoln/Lincoln Memorial
$10 1933-53B Hamilton/Treasury

	F	XF
$1 1928	10.00	25.00
$1 1928A	10.00	25.00
$1 1928B	10.00	27.00
$1 1928C	140.00	3,200.00
$1 1928D	45.00	115.00
$1 1928E	325.00	650.00
$1 1934	13.00	28.00
$1 1935	5.00	9.00
$1 1935A	3.00	5.00
$1 1935A HAWAII	25.00	42.00
$1 1935A yellow seal	22.00	38.00
$1 1935A red R	45.00	100.00
$1 1935A red S	40.00	90.00
$1 1935B	2.50	4.00
$1 1935C	2.50	3.50
$1 1935D	2.00	3.00

	XF	CU
$1 1935E	—	7.00
$1 1935F	—	7.00
$1 1935G	—	8.00
same with motto	4.00	30.00
$1 1935H	—	10.00
$1 1957	—	5.00
$1 1957A	—	6.50
$1 1957B	—	6.50
$5 1934	10.00	34.00
$5 1934A	10.00	20.00
$5 1934A yellow seal	65.00	200.00
$5 1934B	18.00	40.00
$5 1934C	12.00	25.00
$5 1934D	10.00	20.00
$5 1953	—	20.00
$5 1953A	—	16.00
$5 1953B	—	16.00

5 Dollar Small Size Silver Certificate, Special Yellow Seal, 1934A

5 Dollar Small Size Silver Certificate, Blue Seal, Series 1934B

10 Dollar Small Size Silver Certificate, Blue Seal, 1933

10 Dollar Small Size Silver Certificate, Special Yellow Seal, Series 1934A

	XF	CU		XF	CU
$10 1933	6,300.00	12,500.00	$10 1934B	275.00	1,600.00
$10 1933A	—	unique	$10 1934C	45.00	100.00
$10 1934	35.00	95.00	$10 1934D	40.00	150.00
$10 1934A	42.00	125.00	$10 1953	55.00	150.00
$10 1934 yellow seal			$10 1953A	90.00	200.00
	7,000.00	20,000.00	$10 1953B	55.00	125.00
$10 1934A yellow seal					
	85.00	200.00			

FEDERAL RESERVE NOTES

The Federal Reserve System was created in 1913. Under this system there are twelve Federal Reserve Banks. They are governed in part by the U.S. government through the Federal Reserve Board, appointed by the President and confirmed by the Senate. Each of the Federal Reserve Banks is composed of various member banks. Today in the United States, the paper currency is not directly issued by the Treasury, but by the Federal Reserve Banks. Originally Federal Reserve Notes bore an obligation of the government to redeem them in gold. This was changed in 1934. Today Federal Reserve Notes are the only type of paper money issued in the United States.

Just like all other currency, Federal Reserve Notes were reduced in size with the "series of 1928" in 1929.

Since 1993, major new innovations have been gradually incorporated into these notes to prevent counterfeiting. At first micro printing was incorporated into the design and around the frame of the portrait. Also a transparent strip bearing the value and USA was imbedded inside the paper. It can only be seen when the note is held up to the light and cannot be photocopied.

These improvements were only a precursor to the first major overhaul of the designs of the currency since the 1920s. It incorporated these two, as well as other safeguards. Beginning in 1996 with the $100 note the portraits were enlarged to show more detail. The reverse was modified to incorporate more white space, making it possible to successfully use a watermark incorporated into the paper. This is an image neither printed on nor imbedded inside the paper, but one created by the pressure of a pattern pressed against the paper during its drying stage. Like the transparent printed strip, it can only be seen when the note is held up to the light. Among the most ingenious high-tech safeguards on the new notes is the use of color shifting ink, which alters its color depending on the angle of the light hitting it. The green Treasury seal has been retained, but the old letter seal indicating the Federal Reserve Bank of distribution is now replaced by the seal of the Federal Reserve system. These innovations were also incorporated into the 1996 series $50 and $20 notes, with the $10 and $5 notes following during the 1999 series. The $1 note is intended to remain basically the same.

Additional steps were taken to prevent counterfeiting in 2004. Both the $20 and $50 note received multi-color background designs. The change is also scheduled for the $10 in 2005, and for the $100 after $10.

A recent experiment with the use of a Web Press in the manufacture of $1 notes has resulted in less than total success. Interestingly enough for collectors, however, is the fact that this has resulted in some paper money being printed outside the Bureau of Engraving and Printing for the first time since the nineteenth century, and the appearance of an actual mint mark, FW being used to designate Fort Worth, Texas.

Most Federal Reserve Notes since the 1930s are only collected in high grade. Dealers may be unwilling to buy even scarce pieces if not crisp uncirculated. Star replacement notes are quite popularly collected in this series, but again, must usually be crisp to be desirable. Very recent ones command no premium at all, and are sold at face value plus a handling fee to cover the dealer's labor.

Known Counterfeits: Examine detail, silk threads in paper and use reasonable caution. Circulating counterfeits exist, particularly $20, and to a lesser extent the $10. Most are imperfect, and can be easily detected on close examination. The $100 is the most counterfeited outside the United States.

10 Dollar Large Size Federal Reserve Note, Red Seal, Series 1914

	F	XF
RED SEAL—SERIES OF 1914		
$5 Abraham Lincoln/Columbus and Pilgrims	350.00	650.00
$10 Andrew Jackson/reaper and factory	330.00	750.00
$20 Grover Cleveland/train and ship	500.00	1,100.00
$50 Ulysses S. Grant/allegory of Panama	1,200.00	2,250.00
$100 Franklin/five allegories including commerce and agriculture	1,500.00	3,000.00

5 Dollar Large Size Federal Reserve Note, Blue Seal, Series 1914

10 Dollar Large Size Federal Reserve Note, Blue Seal, Series 1914

1,000 Dollar Large Size Federal Reserve Note, Blue Seal, Series 1918

BLUE SEAL—SERIES OF 1914

	F	XF
$5 Abraham Lincoln/Columbus and Pilgrims	55.00	90.00
$10 Andrew Jackson/Reaper and factory	65.00	110.00
$20 Grover Cleveland/train and ship	100.00	150.00
$50 Ulysses S. Grant/allegory of Panama	200.00	460.00
$100 Franklin/five allegories including commerce and agriculture	525.00	700.00

BLUE SEAL—SERIES OF 1918

	F	XF
$500 John Marshall/DeSoto discovering Mississippi	5,000.00	12,000.00
$1,000 Alexander Hamilton/eagle	6,200.00	15,000.00
$5,000 Madison	—	extremely rare
$10,000 Chase	—extremely rare	

SMALL SIZE NOTES—GREEN SEAL

$1 1963 Washington/great seal
$2 1976 Jefferson/Signing Declaration
$5 1928 Lincoln/Lincoln Memorial
$10 1928 Hamilton/Treasury Building
$20 1928 Jackson/White House
$50 1928 Grant/Capitol
$100 1928 Franklin/Independence Hall
$500 1928-34A McKinley/500
$1000 1928-34A Cleveland/inscription
$5000 1928-34B Madison/5000
$10,000 1928-34B Chase/10,000

ONE DOLLAR

	F	XF
$1 1963	—	3.00
$1 1963A	—	3.00
$1 1963B	—	3.50
$1 1969	—	2.50
$1 1969A	—	2.50
$1 1969B	—	2.50
$1 1969C	—	2.50
$1 1969D	—	2.50

5 Dollar Small Size Federal Reserve Note, Green Seal, Series 1928A

	F	XF
$1 1974	—	2.00
$1 1977	—	2.00
$1 1977A	—	2.00
$1 1981	—	2.00
$1 1981A	—	3.00
$1 1985	—	2.00
$1 1988	—	2.50
$1 1988A, DC	—	2.00
$1 1988A, FW	—	2.00
$1 1988A web press	4.00	30.00
$1 1993, DC	—	2.00
$1 1993, FW	—	2.00
$1 1993 web press	3.00	15.00
$1 1995, DC	—	2.00
$1 1995, FW	—	2.00
$1 1995 web press	3.00	15.00
$1 1999, DC	—	2.00
$1 1999, FW	—	2.00
$1 2001, DC	—	2.00
$1 2001, FW	—	2.00
$1 2003, DC	—	2.00
$1 2003, FW	—	2.00

TWO DOLLARS

	XF	CU
$2 1976	—	4.00
$2 1995	—	4.00

FIVE DOLLARS

	XF	CU
$5 1928	35.00	100.00
$5 1928A	25.00	95.00
$5 1928B	25.00	50.00
$5 1928C	220.00	600.00
$5 1928D	1,200.00	2,500.00

5 Dollar Small Size Federal Reserve Note, Green Seal, Series 1950A

	XF	CU		XF	CU
$5 1934	20.00	45.00	$5 1950A	—	20.00
$5 1934A	20.00	30.00	$5 1950B	—	20.00
$5 1934 HAWAII	100.00	450.00	$5 1950C	—	15.00
$5 1934A HAWAII	125.00	450.00	$5 1950D	—	15.00
$5 1934B	20.00	40.00	$5 1950E	—	25.00
$5 1934C	20.00	50.00	$5 1963	—	15.00
$5 1934D	20.00	50.00	$5 1963A	—	12.00
$5 1950	—	45.00			

5 Dollar Small Size Federal Reserve Note, Green Seal, Series 1969

	XF	CU
$5 1969	—	10.00
$5 1969A	—	12.00
$5 1969B	—	35.00
$5 1969C	—	12.00
$5 1974	—	10.00
$5 1977	—	10.00
$5 1977A	—	10.00
$5 1981	—	10.00
$5 1981A	—	10.00

	XF	CU
$5 1985	—	10.00
$5 1988	—	10.00
$5 1988A	—	10.00
$5 1993	—	10.00
$5 1995	—	10.00
$5 1999 large portrait	—	10.00
$5 2001	—	10.00
$5 2003	—	10.00

10 Dollar Small Size Federal Reserve Note, Green Seal, Series 1928

TEN DOLLARS

	XF	CU		XF	CU
$10 1928	60.00	250.00	$10 1934A	15.00	30.00
$10 1928A	60.00	400.00	$10 1934A HAWAII	125.00	500.00
$10 1928B	30.00	75.00	$10 1934B	25.00	75.00
$10 1928C	60.00	350.00	$10 1934C	15.00	30.00
$10 1934	18.00	45.00	$10 1934D	15.00	35.00

10 Dollar Small Size Federal Reserve Note, Green Seal, Series 1950A

	XF	CU		XF	CU
$10 1950	20.00	65.00	$10 1950D	—	35.00
$10 1950A	15.00	35.00	$10 1950E	—	30.00
$10 1950B	—	30.00	$10 1963	—	35.00
$10 1950C	—	35.00	$10 1963A	—	25.00

10 Dollar Small Size Federal Reserve Note, Green Seal, Series 1969

	XF	CU		XF	CU
$10 1969	—	25.00	$10 1969C	—	30.00
$10 1969A	—	25.00	$10 1974	—	25.00
$10 1969B	—	25.00			

10 Dollar Small Size Federal Reserve Note, Green Seal, Series 1977

10 Dollar Small Size Federal Reserve Note, Green Seal, Series 2003

20 Dollar Small Size Federal Reserve Note, Green Seal, Series 1928

TWENTY DOLLARS

	XF	CU		XF	CU
$10 1977	—	30.00	$20 1928	75.00	175.00
$10 1977A	—	25.00	$20 1928A	75.00	300.00
$10 1981	—	35.00	$20 1928B	50.00	100.00
$10 1981A	—	35.00	$20 1928C	750.00	1,500.00
$10 1985	—	25.00			
$10 1988A	—	25.00			
$10 1990	—	15.00			
$10 1993	—	15.00			
$10 1995	—	15.00			
$10 1999 large portrait	—	15.00			
$10 2001	—	15.00			
$10 2003	—	15.00			

20 Dollar Federal Reserve Note, Green Seal, Series 1934

20 Dollar Small Size Federal Reserve Note, Green Seal, Series 1950D

20 Dollar Small Size Federal Reserve Note, Green Seal, Series 1974

	XF	CU		XF	CU
$20 1934	40.00	45.00	$20 1969C	—	45.00
$20 1934A	40.00	60.00	$20 1974	—	45.00
$20 1934 HAWAII	200.00	800.00	$20 1977	—	45.00
$20 1934A HAWAII	100.00	650.00	$20 1981	—	60.00
$20 1934B	35.00	75.00	$20 1981A	—	45.00
$20 1934C	40.00	75.00	$20 1985	—	40.00
$20 1934D	—	45.00	$20 1988A	—	45.00
$20 1950	—	60.00	$20 1990	—	30.00
$20 1950A	—	60.00	$20 1993	—	30.00
$20 1950B	—	45.00	$20 1995	—	30.00
$20 1950C	—	60.00	$20 1996 large portrait	—	30.00
$20 1950D	—	60.00	$20 1999 large portrait	—	25.00
$20 1950E	—	75.00	$20 2001, DC, large portrait	—	25.00
$20 1963	—	60.00	$20 2001, FW, large portrait	—	25.00
$20 1963A	—	45.00	$20 2004, large portrait, colorized background	—	25.00
$20 1969	—	45.00			
$20 1969A	—	50.00			
$20 1969B	—	100.00			

50 Dollar Small Size Federal Reserve Note, Green Seal, Series 1928

FIFTY DOLLARS

	XF	CU		XF	CU
$50 1928	125.00	450.00	$50 1934B	125.00	300.00
$50 1928A	90.00	300.00	$50 1934C	110.00	175.00
$50 1934	75.00	225.00	$50 1934D	75.00	200.00
$50 1934A	90.00	250.00			

50 Dollar Small Size Federal Reserve Note, Green Seal, Series 1950

	XF	CU		XF	CU
$50 1950	70.00	200.00	$50 1950C	65.00	150.00
$50 1950A	70.00	200.00	$50 1950D	60.00	120.00
$50 1950B	60.00	120.00	$50 1950E	200.00	500.00

50 Dollar Small Size Federal Reserve Note, Green Seal, Series 1969A

	XF	CU
$50 1963A	—	100.00
$50 1969	—	150.00
$50 1969A	—	140.00
$50 1969B	—	600.00
$50 1969C	—	100.00
$50 1974	—	100.00
$50 1977	—	80.00
$50 1981	—	125.00
$50 1981A	—	150.00

	XF	CU
$50 1985	—	75.00
$50 1988	—	95.00
$50 1990	—	65.00
$50 1993	—	65.00
$50 1996 large portrait	—	60.00
$50 2001 large portrait	—	60.00
$50 2004 large portrait, colorized background	—	60.00

100 Dollar Small Size Federal Reserve Note, Green Seal, Series 1928A

ONE HUNDRED DOLLARS

	XF	CU
$100 1928	250.00	600.00
$100 1928A	175.00	250.00

100 Dollar Small Size Federal Reserve Note, Green Seal, Series 1934B

	XF	CU		XF	CU
$100 1934	175.00	250.00	$100 1950A	—	200.00
$100 1934A	180.00	300.00	$100 1950B	—	250.00
$100 1934B	400.00	600.00	$100 1950C	—	275.00
$100 1934C	175.00	400.00	$100 1950D	—	250.00
$100 1934D	350.00	450.00	$100 1950E	—	600.00
$100 1950	—	450.00			

100 Dollar Small Size Federal Reserve Note, Green Seal, Series 1963A

	XF	CU
$100 1963A	—	200.00
$100 1969	—	175.00
$100 1969A	—	175.00
$100 1969C	—	175.00
$100 1974	—	150.00
$100 1977	—	175.00
$100 1981	—	200.00
$100 1981A	—	200.00
$100 1985	—	150.00
$100 1988	—	150.00

	XF	CU
$100 1990	—	125.00
$100 1993	—	120.00
$100 1996 large portrait	—	120.00
$100 1999, DC, large portrait	—	120.00
$100 1999, FW, large portrait	—	120.00
$100 2001 large portrait	—	120.00

FIVE HUNDRED DOLLARS

	XF	CU
$500 1928	1,200.00	2,500.00
$500 1934	950.00	1,200.00
$500 1934A	950.00	1,200.00
$500 1934B	550.00	675.00
$500 1934C	550.00	650.00

ONE THOUSAND DOLLARS

	XF	CU
$1000 1928	2,250.00	2,800.00
$1000 1934	2,000.00	2,400.00
$1000 1934A	2,000.00	2,400.00
$1000 1934C	1,250.00	1,500.00

FIVE THOUSAND DOLLARS

	XF	CU
$5000 1928	40,000.00	60,000.00
$5000 1934	35,000.00	50,000.00
$5000 1934A	15,000.00	35,000.00
$5000 1934B	15,000.00	35,000.00

TEN THOUSAND DOLLARS

	XF	CU
$10,000 1928	—	100,000.00
$10,000 1934	—	80,000.00
$10,000 1934A	25,000.00	45,000.00
$10,000 1934B	25,000.00	45,000.00

FEDERAL RESERVE BANK NOTES

Federal Reserve Bank Notes are a type of National Currency issued not by individual National Banks but directly by the twelve Federal Reserve Banks. These are regional banks under the partial control of the Board of Governors of the Federal Reserve, appointed by the President. Unlike Federal Reserve Notes these were legal tender but not a government obligation. The obligation to redeem Federal Reserve Bank Notes fell with the individual Federal Reserve Banks and not directly with the Treasury. They were issued for a fairly short duration.

Small size Federal Reserve Bank Notes are actually emergency currency printed on notes originally intended to become regular 1929 series National Currency. The identity of the Federal Reserve Bank is printed where the name of the National Bank would have been and small details of text are either blocked out or added. They were issued in 1933 and have a brown Treasury seal, unlike the large-size notes, which feature a blue one.

Star replacement notes are scarce and command a significant premium.

Known Counterfeits: Examine detail, silk threads in paper and use reasonable caution.

1 Dollar Large Size Federal Reserve Bank Note, Series 1918

	F	XF
$1 1918 George Washington/eagle on flag	100.00	140.00
$2 1918 Thomas Jefferson/ battleship	365.00	550.00
$5 1915 Abraham Lincoln/Columbus, Pilgrims landing	250.00	450.00
$5 1918 same	250.00	450.00

	F	XF
$10 1915 Andrew Jackson/ horse-drawn reaper and factory	1,100.00	1,750.00
$10 1918 same	1,100.00	1,750.00
$20 1915 Grover Cleveland/train and ship	3,000.00	6,000.00
$20 1918 same	1,350.00	3,000.00
$50 1918 Ulysses S. Grant/allegory of Panama	5,300.00	9,500.00

5 Dollar Small Size Federal Reserve Bank Note, Brown Seal, Series 1929

SMALL-SIZE NOTES—BROWN SEAL

	F	XF
$5 Boston	20.00	50.00
$5 New York	20.00	50.00
$5 Philadelphia	20.00	40.00
$5 Cleveland	20.00	40.00
$5 Atlanta	20.00	50.00
$5 Chicago	15.00	30.00
$5 St. Louis	200.00	600.00
$5 Minneapolis	35.00	150.00
$5 Kansas City	15.00	40.00
$5 Dallas	25.00	60.00
$5 San Francisco	850.00	1,800.00
$10 Boston	20.00	45.00
$10 New York	20.00	45.00
$10 Philadelphia	22.00	50.00
$10 Cleveland	20.00	40.00
$10 Richmond	30.00	65.00
$10 Atlanta	25.00	50.00
$10 Chicago	25.00	45.00
$10 St. Louis	25.00	45.00
$10 Minneapolis	30.00	50.00
$10 Kansas City	25.00	40.00
$10 Dallas	200.00	800.00
$10 San Francisco	30.00	65.00
$20 Boston	28.00	75.00
$20 New York	28.00	50.00
$20 Philadelphia	28.00	50.00
$20 Cleveland	28.00	50.00
$20 Richmond	28.00	50.00
$20 Atlanta	28.00	50.00
$20 Chicago	25.00	40.00
$20 St. Louis	28.00	55.00
$20 Minneapolis	28.00	50.00
$20 Kansas City	28.00	50.00
$20 Dallas	35.00	125.00
$20 San Francisco	60.00	200.00
$50 New York	65.00	110.00
$50 Cleveland	65.00	110.00
$50 Chicago	65.00	100.00

10 Dollar Small Size Federal Reserve Bank Note, Brown Seal, Series 1929

20 Dollar Small Size Federal Reserve Bank Note, Brown Seal, Series 1929

100 Dollar Small Size Federal Reserve Bank Note, Brown Seal, Series 1929

	F	XF		F	XF
$50 Minneapolis	80.00	150.00	$100 Richmond	125.00	200.00
$50 Kansas City	75.00	100.00	$100 Chicago	125.00	175.00
$50 Dallas	150.00	425.00	$100 Minneapolis	125.00	175.00
$50 San Francisco	85.00	150.00	$100 Kansas City	125.00	175.00
$100 New York	125.00	175.00	$100 Dallas	140.00	250.00
$100 Cleveland	135.00	160.00			

CONFEDERATE STATES ISSUES

The story of Confederate paper money is in some ways reminiscent of that of Continental Currency. Under desperate wartime circumstances, and with the best intentions, the government attempted to finance the war effort by printing unbacked paper currency. The initial series, backed by cotton, held its value at first and restraint was used in the quantities issued, but as the war continued more and more were printed, causing inflation. According to the legends on the later notes, they could not be redeemed until "two years after the ratification of a treaty of peace between the Confederate States and United States." Ultimately the seventh and final issue was authorized in unlimited quantity. After two billion dollars were issued, the currency's value eroded almost completely. Measured in gold dollars its decline can be seen as follows, along with rough quantities issued or authorized:

1861 March	$150,000,000	95¢
1862	$265,000,000	
1863	$515,000,000	33¢
1864	$1,000,000,000	
1865 April	none	1-2/3¢
1865 May	none	1/12¢

For many years Confederate currency was synonymous with worthlessness, and some people even burned it. From the 1960s onward it has taken on value as a collectible. Since the late 1990s, there has been a particularly strong market for this series. Prices have increased drastically.

The first issue of Confederate currency of March 1861 was initially issued in Montgomery, Alabama, but the wording was changed to Richmond, Virginia. This is because the capitol of the Confederacy was moved to Richmond in May after Virginia withdrew from the Union. Throughout the war the production of Confederate notes was plagued with difficulties. The Northern printers, who had originally been hired to print notes before hostilities erupted, were no longer available. Paper was in short supply. It was also not always practical to import notes, paper or even plates due to the Union blockade of Southern ports. Some paper was brought in from the North by smugglers and from Great Britain by blockade runners. As a result some of the designs use improvised images not initially prepared for Confederate currency. More suitable images used include portraits of President Jefferson Davis and members of his cabinet, as well as of Southern agriculture.

Known Counterfeits: It has been suggested that contemporary counterfeits were made of virtually every type of Confederate currency. True or false, it stands that a vast array of contemporary counterfeits of Confederate notes have survived. Most are printed from very crudely engraved plates. Like real examples, they are often printed on thin, limp paper. Not all the counterfeits made during the Civil War were actually meant to circulate. Samuel Upham of Philadelphia made 1-1/2 million Confederate and Southern state notes as a spoof, all with the notice "Facsimile Confederate Note—Sold wholesale and retail, by S.C. Upham, 403 Chestnut Street, Philadelphia" in the margin. Many had this notice cut off and intact examples are worth at least a few dollars each. In 1954 Cheerios cereal distributed reproductions as a promotion. Other similar notes printed on brittle brownish-yellow paper were printed in the 1960s. Many but not all have the word FACSIMILE near the margin.

Reproduction One Hundred Dollar Confederate Bill

Some "fantasy" notes were also made to circulate during the Civil War period. These were notes claiming to be Confederate, but with designs which the Confederate government never used. The most famous of these notes is the "female riding a deer" note, which actually depicted Artemis riding a stag. It is illustrated below. Most of the counterfeits, both contemporary and modern, have printed signatures, all authentic notes are hand signed except for the 50¢ denomination.

FIRST ISSUE, MONTGOMERY 1861

	VG	VF
$50 Three slaves hoeing cotton	2,250.00	5,200.00
$100 Train	850.00	4,400.00
$500 Train on bridge, cattle below	1,400.00	8,800.00
$1000 John Calhoun and Andrew Jackson	1,700.00	8,000.00

FIRST ISSUE, RICHMOND 1861

	VG	VF
$50 Industry and Agriculture seated on cotton	110.00	700.00
$100 Train	140.00	750.00

SECOND ISSUE, JULY 25, 1861

	VG	VF
$5 Inscription	250.00	2,100.00
$5 Liberty and eagle, sailor left	220.00	1,600.00
$10 Liberty and eagle, Commerce left	38.00	450.00
$20 Sailing ship	20.00	110.00
$20 Artemis riding stag, Indian seated left, Contemporary Fantasy	18.00	70.00
$50 Washington	22.00	125.00
$100 Ceres and Proserpina	110.00	700.00

THIRD ISSUE, SEPTEMBER 2, 1861

	VG	VF
$2 Confederacy striking down Union, Judah Benjamin l.	90.00	400.00
$5 Cotton being loaded onto steamboat left, Indian princess right	1,300.00	7,750.00
$5 Commerce seated on bale of cotton	17.00	45.00

5 Dollar Commerce Seated on Bale, Third Issue

20 Dollar Industry Seated Behind Large 20, Third Issue

	VG	VF
$5 Allegories of Commerce, Agriculture, Liberty, Industry and Justice, Minerva left	80.00	500.00
$5 Sailor with cotton bales, C.G. Memminger left	32.00	75.00
$5 Boy's bust left, blacksmith seated right	130.00	700.00
$5 C.G. Memminger, V at lower right	15.00	—
same but contempory counterfiet	10.00	—
$5 same, but FIVE at lower right	27.00	85.00
$10 Liberty with eagle left	650.00	4,250.00
$10 Ceres and Commerce left	17.00	75.00
$10 Indian Family	80.00	425.00
$10 Cotton Picker	35.00	200.00
$10 Revolutionary War generals with sweet potatoes, Minerva standing r.	17.00	75.00
$10 Wagon with cotton, John Ward left	200.00	950.00
$10 Robert Hunter left, child right	30.00	150.00
$10 Hope with anchor, Robert Hunter left, C.G. Memminger rt.	22.00	150.00
$10 same, with X X overprint	27.00	125.00
$20 Ceres between Commerce and Navigation	80.00	450.00
$20 Sailing ship	17.00	65.00
$20 Navigation seated with globe	350.00	1,800.00
$20 Industry seated behind large 20	12.00	50.00
$20 Alexander Stephens	40.00	200.00
$50 Moneta & chest	20.00	100.00
$50 Train	450.00	3,600.00
$50 Jefferson Davis	27.00	175.00
$100 Loading cotton onto wagon, sailor left	27.00	100.00

FOURTH ISSUE, APRIL 17, 1862

	VG	VF
$1 Steamship	22.00	100.00
$1 same with ONE overprint	26.00	140.00
$2 Confederacy striking down Union, Judah Benjamin l.	22.00	75.00
$2 same with "2 TWO" overprint	30.00	125.00
$10 Commerce reclining	—	rare
$10 Ceres seated	—	rare
$20 Liberty with shield	650.00	3,600.00
$100 Train	27.00	75.00
$100 Hoeing cotton	27.00	75.00

FIFTH ISSUE, DECEMBER 2, 1862

	VG	VF
$1 Clement Clay	26.00	85.00
$2 Judah Benjamin	24.00	75.00
$5 Confederate capitol at Richmond, Memminger right	12.00	42.00
$10 South Carolina capitol, Robert Hunter right	12.00	42.00
$20 Tennessee capitol, Alexander Stephens right	22.00	110.00
$50 Jefferson Davis	27.00	150.00
$100 Lucy Pickens	35.00	150.00

SIXTH ISSUE, APRIL 6, 1863

	VG	VF
50¢ Jefferson Davis	12.00	38.00
$1 Clement Clay	25.00	85.00
$2 Judah Benjamin	25.00	175.00
$5 Confederate capitol at Richmond, Memminger right	20.00	38.00
$10 South Carolina capitol, Robert Hunter right	18.00	45.00
$20 Tennessee capitol, Alexander Stephens right	16.00	50.00
$50 Jefferson Davis	22.00	75.00
$100 Lucy Pickens center, soldiers left, George Randolph right	27.00	85.00

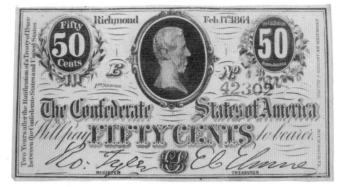

50 Cent Jefferson Davis, Seventh Issue

10 Dollar Field Artillery, Robert Hunter Right, Seventh Issue

SEVENTH ISSUE, FEBRUARY 17, 1864

	VG	VF
50¢ Jefferson Davis	10.00	35.00
$1 Clement Clay	32.00	110.00
$2 Judah Benjamin	27.00	85.00
$5 Confederate capitol at Richmond, Memminger right	10.00	35.00
$10 Field Artillery, Robert Hunter right	10.00	30.00
$20 Tennessee capitol, Alexander Stephens right	10.00	30.00

Jefferson Davis 50 Dollar Confederate Note, Seventh Issue

	VG	VF
$50 Jefferson Davis	22.00	65.00
$100 Lucy Pickens, soldiers left, George Randolph right	27.00	70.00
$500 Flag and seal left, Stonewall Jackson right	130.00	450.00

Resources

CLUBS AND ASSOCIATIONS

Coin collecting can be an extremely social hobby, with national, regional and local clubs. The largest numismatic organization in the world is the American Numismatic Association. It is an institution chartered by Congress to promote numismatic knowledge, and has over the years attracted hundreds of thousands of collectors and dealers. Not only does it provide the arbitration services mentioned above, but holds large conventions twice each year at various locations throughout the country. The summer A.N.A. convention is particularly important being one of the largest coin shows in the world, including not only coin dealers but also representatives of the mints of many foreign countries. Other benefits to A.N.A. membership include a circulating numismatic library, access to its one-week summer seminar in Colorado, and an authentication service. Every member of the A.N.A. also receives a monthly issue of the Numismatist, its official journal containing many popular articles and columns, as well as ads by member dealers. Its address is:

> American Numismatic Association
> 818 North Cascade Ave.
> Colorado Springs, CO 80903
> www.money.org.

Another extremely important institution is the American Numismatic Society, which boasts the most important numismatic library in the Western Hemisphere. It has played a significant role in the promotion of original academic numismatic research, and there is little cutting edge scholarship in which its books or staff are not consulted. It also conducts a summer seminar for graduate students and scholarships for students incorporating numismatic research in their theses. Its address is:

American Numismatic Society
96 Fulton Street
New York, NY 10038 in the Financial District
www.numismatics.org.

Many regional associations exist, and most of them sponsor important coin shows. One of the largest such organizations is F.U.N. or Florida United Numismatists, which sponsors a large show of national importance each January in Orlando. Another large regional organization is the Central States Numismatic Association which sponsors conventions throughout the Midwest. The addresses of some of the more important regional societies are:

Florida United Numismatists
POB 951988
Lake Mary, FL 32795

Central States Numismatic Society
POB 841
Logansport, IN 46947

Great Eastern Numismatic Association
1805 Weatherstone Drive
Paoli, PA 19301

New England Numismatic Association
POB 586
Needham, MA 02192

Pacific Northwest Numismatic Association
P.O. Box 4718
Federal Way, WA 98063-4718

There are, of course, a good many state level organizations, too numerous to mention here.

There is also a good chance that there is a local coin club which meets regularly in your town or county. There are hundreds of such organizations throughout the United States. Instead of at coin shows, most get together in a more low-key and informal manner. Many such organizations are members of the A.N.A. themselves, and contacting the A.N.A. may be one way of getting in touch with one. Also ask at your local library or coin shop.

MUSEUMS

There is nothing for getting acquainted with numismatics like viewing the exhibits presented by a numismatic museum. It is an experience no beginner will soon forget. There are only two purely numismatic museums in the United States, but others also have respectable coin collections and numismatic exhibits. Both the American Numismatic Association in Colorado Springs and the American Numismatic Society in New York have very important museums with public exhibits of coins. (The A.N.S. exhibit is temporarily located at the nearby Federal Reserve Bank of New York while the museum renovates its new building.) The exhibits at either institution will give a good overview of the evolution of coinage and money over the last couple thousand years.

For decades the Smithsonian Institution in Washington, D.C. also has had a very significant numismatic collection on display, with notable pieces in the fields of United States and world gold, as well as of Russian coinage, among others. Recently it announced its intention to shut down its coin display in the near future. Some coins will be featured on its Web site, www.si.edu.

Almost all museums have 99% of their holding stored in secure vaults, with selected representative coins on display. Museum curators are notably cooperative with scholars and serious collectors, however, and a call to the museum in advance can often arrange for the viewing of specimens not available to the general public.

Non-numismatic institutions with significant coin and/or paper money exhibits include the Federal Reserve Bank of New York (New York, NY) and the Durham Western Heritage Museum (Omaha, Nebraska).

Another way to see fairly interesting coins at a museum is to catch them in interdisciplinary exhibits. One good example was an exhibit of medieval armor mounted by the Metropolitan Museum of Art in New York. Accompanying the suits of armor were large medieval bracteate silver coins depicting similar armor in a contemporary manner. Other museums, including the Smithsonian, have followed this method of exhibiting too.

BOOKS ABOUT U.S. COINS

One cannot overemphasize the importance of books in fully understanding rare coins. The difference between a person accumulating a few interesting coins and a true numismatist is not how much a person spends, but how much a person learns.

The following books provide a good general background to U.S. coins. Those books dealing with particular coin series are sequenced in the same order in which series are sequenced in this book. (However, for the readers' benefit, other books are included about coins not covered in this book.) Don't be put off by early publication dates, as many standard works from earlier decades have been reprinted many times and are widely available through coin dealers. This is just a sampling; many other worthwhile books are available.

GENERAL U.S. COIN BOOKS

Berman, Allen G., *Warman's Coins and Paper Money*, 3rd Ed. An expanded version of this book, also including ancients and world coins.

Bowers, Q. David, *The History of United States Coinage As Illustrated by the Garrett Collection.*

Breen, Walter, *Walter Breen's Complete Encyclopedia of U.S. and Colonial Coins.* One of the most intelligent in-depth general catalogs of the series. Excellent!

Breen, Walter, *Walter Breen's Encyclopedia of U.S. and Colonial Proof Coins.*

Fivaz, Bill and Stanton, J.T., *The Cherry Pickers' Guide to Rare Die Varieties.*

Yeoman, R.S., *A Guide Book of United States Coins.* Popularly called the "Red Book," it is the widely acknowledged Bible of U.S. coins.

Yeoman, R.S., *Handbook of United States Coins.* Popularly called the "Blue Book," a companion to the Red Book above, designed for those with an eye to selling their coins.

GRADING

American Numismatic Association, *Official A.N.A. Grading Standards for United States Coins.* No one has any business investing in U.S. coins, or even spending significant money on them as a hobby, if they don't have this book.

Professional Coin Grading Service, *Official Guide to Coin Grading and Counterfeit Detection.*

Ruddy, James F., *Photograde.*

DETECTING COUNTERFEITS

American Numismatic Association, *Counterfeit Detection*, 2 vols.

Fivaz, Bill, Bill Fivaz's *Counterfeit Detection Guide*. Convenient set of blow-up photos of authentic examples by a noted coin photographer.

Harshe, Bert, *How to Detect Altered & Counterfeit Coins and Paper Money*.

Kleeberg, John M., ed., *Circulating Counterfeits of the Americas*, American Numismatic Society, NY.

Larson, Charles M., *Numismatic Forgery*.

Lonesome, John, *Detecting Counterfeit Coins*.

Lonesome, John, *Detecting Counterfeit Gold Coins*.

Professional Coin Grading Service, *Official Guide to Coin Grading and Counterfeit Detection*.

Virtually every issue of *The Numismatist*, the official journal of the A..N.A., has large clear photographs of newly discovered counterfeits.

COLONIAL COINS

Breen, Walter, *Walter Breen's Complete Encyclopedia of U.S. and Colonial Coins*. Despite being a general book, it is also one of the best treatments of Colonials as well.

Crosby, S.S., *The Early Coins of America*.

Kleeberg, John, *Money of Pre-Federal America*.

Maris, Edward, *A Historical Sketch of the Coins of New Jersey*.

Miller, Henry Clay, *State Coinages of Connecticut*.

Newman, Eric P., ed., *Studies on Money in Early America*.

Noe, Sydney, *The New England and Willow Tree Coinage of Massachusetts*.

Noe, Sydney, *The Oak Tree Coinage of Massachusetts*.

Noe, Sydney, *The Pine Tree Coinage of Massachusetts*.

Richardson, A.D., *The Copper Coins of Vermont*. (An extension of the standard numbering system established in Ryder, Hillyer, *The Colonial Coins of Vermont*).

Vlack, Robert, *Early American Coins*.

HALF CENTS

Breen, W., *Walter Breen's Encyclopedia of United States Half Cents 1793-1857*.

Cohen, Roger, *American Half Cents, The "Little Half Sisters."* Establishes a standard numbering system for die varieties.

LARGE CENTS

Newcomb, H., *United States Copper Cents 1816-1857*. (Covers die varieties).

Sheldon, William, *Penny Whimsy*, 1958. (Covers die varieties 1793 to 1815, a standard which has lived through many reprints).

SMALL CENTS

Snow, *Flying Eagle and Indian Cents*.

Taylor, *The Standard Guide to the Lincoln Cent*.

Wiles, James, *The RPM Book—Lincoln Cents*. Guide to repunched mint mark varieties.

TWO-CENT AND THREE-CENT PIECES

Bowers, Q. David, *U.S. Three-Cent and Five-Cent Pieces*.

Flynn, Kevin, *Getting Your Two Cents Worth*.

Kilman, M., *The Two Cent Piece and Varieties, 1977*.

HALF DIMES AND NICKELS

Blythe, Al, *The Complete Guide to Liberty Seated Half Dimes*.

Bowers, Q. David, *U.S. Three-Cent and Five-Cent Pieces*.

Lange, David, *The Complete Guide to Buffalo Nickels*.

Valentine, D.W., *The United States Half Dimes*, 1931. Standard reference on die varieties for the series.

Wescott, Michael, *The United States Nickel Five-Cent Piece*.

DIMES

Bowers, Q. David, *United States Dimes, Quarters, and Half Dollars*.

Greer, Brian, *The Complete Guide to Liberty Seated Dimes*.

Lange, David W., *The Complete Guide to Mercury Dimes*.

Lawrence, David, *The Complete Guide to Barber Dimes*.

Rapsus, Ginger, *The United States Clad Coinage*.

TWENTY-CENT PIECES AND QUARTERS

Bowers, Q. David, *United States Dimes, Quarters, and Half Dollars*.

Briggs, Larry, *Liberty Seated Quarters*.

Browning, A. W., *The Early Quarter Dollars of the United States*. Standard reference on die varieties for the series.

Cline, J.H., *Standing Liberty Quarters*

Hammer, Ted, "The Twenty Cent Piece," *The Numismatist*, vol. 60, pp. 167-69.

Lawrence, David, *The Complete Guide to Barber Quarters.*
Rapsus, Ginger, *The United States Clad Coinage.*

HALF DOLLARS
Bowers, Q. David, *United States Dimes, Quarters and Half Dollars.*
Fox, Bruce, *The Complete Guide to Walking Liberty Half Dollars.*
Lawrence, David, *The Complete Guide to Barber Halves.*
Overton, Al C., *Early Half Dollar Die Varieties 1794-1836.* Standard reference on die varieties for the series.
Rapsus, Ginger, *The United States Clad Coinage.*

SILVER & CLAD DOLLARS
Bolender, M.H., *The United States Early Silver Dollars from 1794 to 1803.* Standard reference on die varieties for the series.
Bowers, Q. David, *Silver Dollars and Trade Dollars of the United States: A Complete Encyclopedia.*
Newman, Eric, and Bressett, Kenneth, *The Fantastic 1804 Dollar.*
Rapsus, Ginger, *The United States Clad Coinage.*
Van Allen, Leroy, and Mallis, A. George, *Comprehensive Catalogue and Encyclopedia of U.S. Morgan and Peace Silver Dollars.*
Willem, John M., *The United States Trade Dollar.*

GOLD COINAGE
Akers, David, *Handbook of 20th-Century United States Gold Coins.*
Bowers, Q. David, *United States Gold Coins: An Illustrated History.*

COMMEMORATIVES
Bowers, Q. David, *Commemorative Coins of the United States: A Complete Encyclopedia.*
Hodder, Michael and Bowers, Q. David, *A Basic Guide to United States Commemorative Coins.*
Swiatek, Anthony and Breen, Walter, *Encyclopedia of United States Silver and Gold Commemorative Coins 1892-1989.*

PROOFS
Breen, Walter, *Walter Breen's Encyclopedia of United States and Colonial Proof Coins.*

PATTERNS
Judd, J. Hewett, *United States Pattern, Experimental and Trial Pieces*. The newest edition of this standard has been updated by Q. David Bowers.

Krause, Chester, and Mishler, Clifford, *Standard Catalog of World Coins* and *Standard Catalog of World Coins, 19th Century*.

ERRORS
Margolis, Arnold, *Error Coin Encyclopedia*.

Spadone, Frank, *Major Variety and Oddity*.

Wiles, James, and Miller, Tom, *The RPM Book*. Guide to repunched mint mark varieties.

TOKENS
Alpert, Stephen and Smith, Kenneth E., *Video Arcade, Pinball, Slot Machine, and other Amusement Tokens of North America*.

Breen, Walter, *Pioneer and Fractional Gold*.

Coffee, John, and Ford, Harold, *Atwood-Coffee Catalogue of United States and Canadian Transportation Tokens*, 5th ed.

Fuld, George and Melvin, *Patriotic Civil War Tokens*.

Fuld, George and Melvin, *U. S. Civil War Store Cards*.

Hibler, Harold and Kappen, Charles, *So-Called Dollars*. A standard work on dollar sized tokens or medals, particularly those used temporarily as a medium of exchange or to represent such satirically.

Hodder, Michael J. and Bowers, Q. David, *Standard Catalogue of Encased Postage Stamps*.

Kagin, Donald, *Private Gold Coins and Patterns of the United States*.

Rulau, Russell, *Standard Catalog of United States Tokens*.

Rulau R. and Fuld, G., *Medallic Portraits of Washington*.

Schenkman, David, *Civil War Suttler Tokens and Cardboard Scrip*.

Sullivan, Edmund B., *American Political Badges and Medalets 1789-1892*.

Token and Medal Society, *TAMS Journal*. The journal of this organization is incredibly useful, with regular listing identifying "mavericks," or private tokens which bear no specific indication of their origin.

HAWAII, ALASKA, U.S. PHILIPPINES
Basso, Aldo, *Coins, Medals and Tokens of the Philippines*.

Gould, Maurice, *Hawaiian Coins, Tokens and Paper Money*.

Krause & Mishler, *Standard Catalog of World Coins*
Yeoman, R.S., *Guidebook of United States Coins*

CONFEDERATE COINS
Reed, Fred L., III, series of articles, *Coin World*, Oct. 4, Oct. 11, Oct. 18, 1989

PERIODICALS ABOUT U.S. COINS

Magazines have a certain immediacy not possible in books. They also put the reader in touch with the opinions of fellow numismatists.

CoinAge (monthly)—A popular newsstand magazine, oriented to the collector and the layman.

Coin Prices (6 per year)—Extensive listings of United States coin values in many grades. Articles more oriented towards the market than towards history. Published by F + W Publications, the world's largest numismatic publisher.

Coins (monthly)—Very similar to *CoinAge* but put out by F + W Publications, the world's largest numismatic publisher.

Coin Values (monthly)—Extensive listings of United States coin values in many grades. Published by *Coin World*.

Coin World (weekly)—The largest circulation coin newspaper, covering both American and world coins.

Counterfeit Coin Bulletin (three times per year)—Detailed reports on newly discovered counterfeits. A joint publication of the American Numismatic Association and the International Association of Professional Numismatists.

Numismatic News (weekly)—An F + W Publications newspaper focusing primarily on United States coins.

The Numismatist (monthly)—The monthly journal of the American Numismatic Association. All full members receive a subscription.

BOOKS ABOUT U.S.
PAPER MONEY

Berman, Allen G., *Warman's Coins & Paper Money, Identification and Price Guide*, 3rd ed.

Eldler, Joel, ed. *Standard Catalog of United States Paper Money*, 25th ed.

Edler, Joel, ed., *Standard Guide to Small Size U.S. Paper Money: 1928 to Date*, 7th ed.

Lee, Wallace G., *Michigan 19th Century Obsolete Bank & Scrip Notes/ National Bank Notes 1863-1935*.

Newman, Eric P., *The Early Paper Money of America: Colonial Currency 1696-1810*, 5th ed.

Index

COINS BY DENOMINATION

1/2 Cent, 36-39

1 Cent
Flying Eagle Cents, 44
Indian Head Cents, 45-47
Large Cents, 39-44
Lincoln Cents, 47-53

2 Cents, 54

3 Cents
Nickel Three-Cent Pieces, 57
Silver Three-Cent Pieces, 55-56

5 Cents
Buffalo Nickels, 61-63
Bust Half Dimes, 68-70
Jefferson Nickels, 64-68
Liberty Nickels, 59-60
Seated Liberty Half Dimes, 70-72
Shield Nickels, 58

10 Cents
Barber Dimes, 78-79
Bust Dimes, 73-74
Mercury Dimes, 80-82
Roosevelt Dimes, 82-85
Seated Liberty Dimes, 75-77

20 Cents, 85

25 Cents
Barber Quarters, 92-93
Bust Quarters, 86-88
Seated Liberty Quarters, 88-92
Standing Liberty Quarters, 94-96
State Quarters, 101-110
Washington Quarters, 96-100

50 Cents
Barber Half Dollars, 120-120
Early Half Dollars, 111-115
Franklin Half Dollars, 125-126
Kennedy Half Dollars, 126-129
Seated Liberty Half Dollars, 115-120

Walking Liberty Half Dollars, 123-124

1 Dollar
Early Silver Dollars, 130-132
Eisenhower Dollars, 142-143
Gobrecht Dollars, 132-133
Morgan Dollars, 137-140
Peace Dollars, 141-142
Sacagawea Dollars, 145-146
Seated Liberty Dollars, 134-136
Susan B. Anthony Dollars, 144
Trade Dollars, 136-137

Gold Dollar
Coronet, 147-148
Large Indian Princess Head, 149
Narrow Indian Princess Head, 148

Gold 2-1/2 Dollars (Quarter Eagle)
Capped Bust, 152
Classic Head, 152
Coronet, 153-155
Indian Head, 156
Turban Bust, 151

Gold 3 Dollars, 157

Gold 5 Dollars (Half Eagle)
Capped Bust, 160-161
Classic Head, 161
Coronet, 162-165
Indian Head, 166
Turban Bust, 159-160

Gold 10 Dollars (Eagle)
Coronet, 169-172
Indian Head, 172-173
Turban Bust, 168

Gold 20 Dollars (Double Eagle)
Liberty Head, 175-178
St. Gaudens, 178-179

PAPER MONEY BY ISSUE

Confederate States Issues, 250-257
Demand Notes, 192-193
Federal Reserve Notes, 225-245
Federal Reserve Bank Notes, 246-250
Gold Certificates, 213-216
National Bank Notes, 196-204
National Gold Bank Notes, 205
Silver Certificates, 217-224
Treasury Notes, 194-196
United States Notes, 206-212

ALPHABETICAL LISTING

A

Associations, 258-259

B

Barber Dimes, 78-79
Barber Half Dollars, 120-122
Barber Quarters, 92-93
Books
    Coin, 262-267
    Paper Money, 268
Buffalo Nickels, 61-63
Bust Dimes, 73-74
Bust Half Dimes, 68-70
Bust Quarters, 86-88

C

Cleaning Coins, 26
Clubs, 259
Confederate States Issues, 250-257
Counterfeits, Paper Money, 190-192

D

Demand Notes, 192-193
Double Eagles, 173-179

E

Eagles, 166-173
Early Half Dollars, 111-115
Early Silver Dollars, 130-132
Eisenhower Dollars, 142-143
Errors, Coins, 30-35

F

Federal Reserve Bank Notes, 246-250
Federal Reserve Notes, 225-245
Flying Eagle Cents, 44
Franklin Half Dollars, 125-126

G

Gobrecht Dollars, 132-133
Gold Certificates, 213-216
Grading,
    Coins, 15-23
    Paper Money, 189

H

Half Cents, 36-39
Half Eagles, 158-166
Handling,
    Coins, 26
    Paper Money, 190

I

Indian Head Cents, 45-47

J

Jefferson Nickels, 64-68

K

Kennedy Half Dollars, 126-129

L

Large Cents, 39-44
Liberty Nickels, 59-60
Lincoln Cents, 47-53

M

Mercury Dimes, 80-82
Mints, 14
Mint Marks, 14
Mint Sets, 184-187
Morgan Dollars, 137-140
Museums, 261

N

National Bank Notes, 196-204
National Gold Bank Notes, 205
Nickel Three-Cent Pieces, 57

O

Online Collecting, 28

P

Peace Dollars, 141-142
Periodicals, Coin, 267
Proof Sets, 180-183

Q

Quarter Eagles, 150-156

R

Resources, 258-268
Roosevelt Dimes, 82-85

S

Sacagawea Dollars, 145-146
Seated Liberty Dimes, 75-77
Seated Liberty Dollars, 134-136
Seated Liberty Half Dimes, 70-72
Seated Liberty Half Dollars, 115-120
Seated Liberty Quarters, 88-92
Shield Nickels, 58
Silver Certificates, 217-224
Silver Three-Cent Pieces, 55-56
Slabs, 24-25
St. Gaudens 20 Dollar Gold Pieces,
  178-179

Standing Liberty Quarters, 94-96
State Quarters, 101-110
Storage of Coins, 26-27
Susan B. Anthony Dollars, 144

T

Trade Dollars, 136-137
Treasury Notes, 194-196
Twenty-Cent Pieces, 85

U

United States Notes, 206-212

W

Walking Liberty Half Dollars, 123-124
Washington Quarters, 96-100

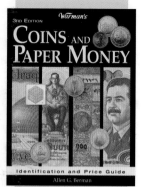